Communications in Computer and Information Science 1703

More information about this series at https://link.springer.com/bookseries/7899

Arthur Gibadullin (Ed.)

Information Technologies and Intelligent Decision Making Systems

First International Conference, ITIDMS 2021
Virtual Event, January 25, 2021
Revised Selected Papers

Springer

Editor
Arthur Gibadullin
National Research University Moscow Power
Engineering Institute
Moscow, Russia

ISSN 1865-0929   ISSN 1865-0937 (electronic)
Communications in Computer and Information Science
ISBN 978-3-031-21339-7   ISBN 978-3-031-21340-3 (eBook)
https://doi.org/10.1007/978-3-031-21340-3

This Springer imprint is published by the registered company Springer Nature Switzerland AG
The registered company address is: Gewerbestrasse 11, 6330 Cham, Switzerland

Preface

The International Scientific and Practical Conference "Information Technologies and Intelligent Decision Making Systems" (ITIDMS 2021) was held on January 25, 2021, on the Microsoft Teams platform due to COVID-19.

The conference was held with the aim of summarizing international experience in the field of information, digital, and intellectual development, within which proposals were formulated for digital and information transformation and the development of computer models, information technologies, and automated and computing processes.

A distinctive feature of the conference is that authors from China, Uzbekistan, Lebanon, Poland, Kazakhstan, Bulgaria, and Russia presented their work. Researchers from different countries addressed the process of information transition and the digital path of development, highlighting the main directions and research activities that can improve efficiency and development.

The conference sessions were moderated by Gibadullin Artur Arturovich of the National Research University "Moscow Power Engineering Institute", Moscow, Russia.

The Organizing Committee decided not to postpone the conference, even though COVID-19 was gaining momentum, and instead the conference took place virtually at the appointed time.

Thus, the conference still facilitated scientific recommendations on the use of information, computer, digital, and intellectual technologies in industry and fields of activity that can be useful to state and regional authorities, international and supranational organizations, and the scientific and professional community.

Each presented paper was reviewed by at least three members of Program Committee in a double-blind manner. As a result of the work of all reviewers, 13 papers were accepted for publication out of the 41 received submissions. The reviews were based on the assessment of the topic of the submitted materials, the relevance of the study, the scientific significance and novelty, the quality of the materials, and the originality of the work. Authors could revise their paper and submit it again for review. Reviewers, Program Committee members, and Organizing Committee members did not enter into discussions with the authors of the articles.

The Organizing Committee of the conference expresses its gratitude to the staff at Springer who supported the publication of this proceedings. In addition, the Organizing Committee would like to thank the conference participants, reviewers, and everyone who helped organize this conference and shape the present volume for publication in the Springer CCIS series.

Gibadullin Artur Arturovich

Organization

Program Committee Chairs

Gulyaev Yuri Vasilievich	Institute of Radio-engineering and Electronics, RAS, Russia
Zernov Vladimir Alekseevich	Russian New University, Russia
Kryukovskiy Andrey Sergeevich	Russian New University, Russia
Palkin Evgeny Alekseevich	Russian New University, Russia
Gibadullin Artur Arturovich	National Research University "Moscow Power Engineering Institute", Russia

Program Committee

Bovtrikova Elena Vladislavovna	Russian New University, Russia
Bugaev Alexander Stepanovich	Institute of Radio-engineering and Electronics, RAS, Russia
Gladyshev Anatoly Ivanovich	Russian New University, Russia
Dongxiao (Mike) Gu	Hefei University of Technology, China
Uzakov Gulom	Karshi Engineering and Economic Institute, Uzbekistan
Shvetsova Olga	Korea University of Technology and Education, South Korea
Zolotarev Oleg Vasilievich	Russian New University, Russia
Kalinina Maria Anatolyevna	Russian New University, Russia
Labunets Leonid Vitalievich	Russian New University, Russia
Morkovkin Dmitry Evgenievich	Financial University under the Government of the Russia, Russia
Oleinikov Alexander Yakovlevich	Institute of Radio-engineering and Electronics, RAS, Russia
Saidzoda Rahimjon Khamro	National Research Technological University MISiS, Dushanbe, Tajikistan
Sadriddinov Mahmadi Makhmudovich	Tajik Technical University named after academician M.S. Osimi, Tajikistan
Sadriddinov Manuchehr Islomiddinovich	Tajik State University of Finance and Economics, Tajikistan
Seyed Komail Tayebi	University of Isfahan, Iran
Pritish Kumar Varadwaj	Indian Institute of Information Technology, Allahabad, India
Pulyaeva Valentina Nikolaevna	Financial University under the Government of the Russia, Russia

Rastyagaev Dmitry Vladimirovich   Russian New University, Russia

Organizing Committee

Gibadullin Artur Arturovich	National Research University "Moscow Power Engineering Institute", Russia
Bovtrikova Elena Vladislavovna	Russian New University, Russia
Agapov Yuri Petrovich	Russian New University, Russia
Guskov Boris Leonidovich	Russian New University, Russia
Matyunina Olga Evgenievna	Russian New University, Russia
Mikhaleva Elizaveta Vyacheslavovna	Russian New University, Russia
Morkovkin Dmitry Evgenievich	Financial University under the Government of the Russia, Moscow, Russia
Pulyaeva Valentina Nikolaevna	Financial University under the Government of the Russia, Russia
Rastyagaev Dmitry Vladimirovich	Russian New University, Russia

Organizer

Russian New University, Russia

Contents

Analysis of Domain Name Resolution Strategy of Local DNS Server in the Transition from IPv4 to IPv6

Qingyuan Shan[✉] [ID]

Dalian Polytechnic University, Dalian 116034, Liaoning, China
shanqy@dlpu.edu.cn

Abstract. To better control the domain name publishing effect of authorized DNS server during the transition from IPv4 to IPv6, the resolution strategy of local DNS server needs to be analyzed. Through differentiated release of the A and AAAA record of 4 domain names on IPv4 and IPv6 authorized DNS servers, and 6 common and representative local DNS servers were set to resolve each test domain name 10 times a day for a total of 10 days. The results are statistically analyzed to infer the resolution strategy of each local DNS server to be tested. Through the research of local DNS server resolution strategy, the conclusion is that any domain name needs to be published simultaneously in the DNS IPv4 and IPv6 authorized servers to ensure that Internet users can obtain correct resolution results of the domain name in each resolution.

Keywords: IPv4 · IPv6 · Local Dns Server · Authorized Dns Server · Dns resolution strategy

1 Introduction

With the depletion of IPv4 address resources and the transition to IPv6 network, the state vigorously promotes the deployment of IPv6, and more and more websites need to be published on IPv6 network. For the IPv6 address is longer and more complex, it is almost impossible for ordinary users to access the website through the IPv6 address. Therefore, it is necessary to resolve the domain name to IPv6 address (AAAA record) first [1].

Domain names can be published on DNS IPv4 authorized server, IPv6 authorized server, or both. When we do this, we may use the transition technology from IPv4 to IPv6, such as NAT64 [2–4] or DNS64 [5]. Domain name must be published through the authorized DNS server, but few internet users obtain resolution directly by the authorized DNS server, usually they use the local DNS server. Therefore, the resolution strategy of the local DNS server will have an impact on users' obtaining resolution results, especially in the current transition process from IPv4 to IPv6.

The six public local DNS servers commonly used in China can fully reflect the resolution strategy of the current local DNS server. The differentiated release of the four test domain names on IPv4 and IPv6 DNS authorized servers can clearly find the source

A. Gibadullin (Ed.): ITIDMS 2021, CCIS 1703, pp. 1–11, 2022.
https://doi.org/10.1007/978-3-031-21340-3_1

of resolution obtained by the local DNS server, and the DNS test tools can fully find the settings behind the local DNS server.

2   Public Local DNS Server

Internet users obtain AAAA and A records of relevant domain names through local DNS servers. Generally, when users use the network service, operators will dynamically allocate network parameters such as IP address and local DNS server address to users. There are three operators: China Unicom, mobile and Telecom. In addition, to meet the diversified needs of users for local DNS servers, some companies have set up free local DNS servers, such as 114dns in China and Google DNS abroad. Some common public local DNS servers are selected for test, as shown in Table 1:

Table 1. Common public local DNS server

Local DNS server IPv4	PTR record	Operator
8.8.8.8	dns.google	USAGoogle
114.114.114.114	public1.114dns.com	ChinaGreatbit
202.38.184.13	CS.NIC.EDU.CN	ChinaCERNET
202.96.69.38	dns.dl.lnpta.net.cn	ChinaUnicom
211.137.32.178	liaoning-chinamobile-dns.ln.chinamobile.com	China Mobile
219.149.6.99	dns2.lntele.com	ChinaTelecom

3   Differentiated Domain Name Publishing

The domain names to be tested are published simultaneously in IPv4 and IPv6 authorized DNS servers, and different databases are used, such as domain name itins4.dlpu.edu.cn's A and AAAA records are only published in the IPv4 authorized DNS server, and there are no A and AAAA records corresponding to the domain name in the IPv6 authorized server's database; Instead, itins6.dlpu.edu.cn's A and AAAA records are only published in the IPv6 authorized DNS server, and there is no domain name information in the IPv4 authorized server; The databases of IPv4 and IPv6 authorized DNS server are shown in Table 2:

For ease of expression, the domain names and record types of NO 1 to 3 in Table 2 are combined and abbreviated below. For example, 1A represents domain names itins dlpu.edu.cn's A record, 1AAAA represents the domain name itins.dlpu.edu.cn's AAAA record, and so on. Since the fourth domain name in Table 2 is in both IPv4 and IPv6 databases, 4A1 is used to represent itinsa.dlpu.edu.cn's A record in IPv4 authorized server, 4A2 represents itinsa.dlpu.edu.cn A record in IPv6 authorized server. 4AAAA1 represents itinsa.dlpu.edu.cn AAAA record in IPv4 authorized server, 4AAAA2 represents itinsa.dlpu.edu.cn AAAA record in IPv6 authorized server.

Table 2. Authorized DNS server database

No	Domain name	IPv4 authorized DNS server database content	IPv4 authorized DNS server database content
1	itins.dlpu.edu.cn	192.168.0.1	2001:da8:a802:100a::C0A8:0001
2	itins4.dlpu.edu.cn	192.168.0.1 2001:da8:a802:100a::C0A8:0001	no record
3	itins6.dlpu.edu.cn	no record	192.168.0.1 2001:da8:a802:100a::C0A8:0001
4	itinsA.dlpu.edu.cn	192.168.0.1 2001:da8:a802:100a::C0A8:0001	192.168.0.2 2001:da8:a802:100a::C0A8:0002

4 Test Topology

As shown in Fig. 1:

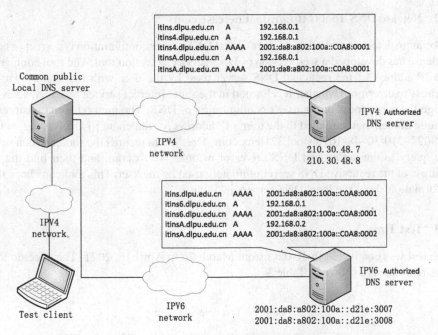

Fig. 1. Test topologyю

5   Test Tools and Time

5.1   Test Tool:DiG 9.3.2

Test command: dig @DNS_server_IP NS_record_type
Such as: dig @8.8.8.8 itins.dlpu.edu.cn a
Send a Query to 8.8.8.8 for the A record of itins.dlpu.edu.cn

If the query is successful, the server returns the A record, such as:
;; flags: qrrdra; QUERY: 1, ANSWER: 1, AUTHORITY: 0, ADDITIONAL: 0
;; ANSWER SECTION:
itins.dlpu.edu.cn.   21599   IN   A   192.168.0.1

If there is'nt corresponding record in database, the server will return the SOA record:
;; flags: qrrdra; QUERY: 1, ANSWER: 0, AUTHORITY: 1, ADDITIONAL: 0
;; AUTHORITY SECTION:
dlpu.edu.cn.   1799   IN   SOA   ns1.dlpu.edu.cn.   Webmaster.dlpu.edu.cn.
2021032601 10800 1800 259200 86400

5.2   Netease DNS Tool (http://nstool.netease.com)

In order to determine whether the user's local DNS server configuration is correct or not, Netease has developed a web version of DNS service detection tool, The tool compares the IP address of the recursive DNS server used by the user with the user's own IP address to determine whether it is located in the same Internet service provider, so as to judge the correctness of the user's configuration of DNS. The method is to construct a unique domain name related to the user's IP address for the client to resolve, e.g. only-388027–210-30–48-167.nstool.321fenx.com. The system records the server which send the query to the authorized DNS server of nstool.321fenx.com, and then find the IP address of the recursive DNS server ultimately used by the user. This tool can check the information about the local DNS servers in Table 1.

5.3   Test Time

The test was conducted in 10 days from March 26 to April 16, 2021. The specific test date and time are shown in Table 3

Table 3. Test date and time

| 20210326–11:06 | 20210329–08:35 | 20210331–15:09 | 20210401–11:17 | 20210402–13:50 |
| 20210406–09:17 | 20210407–10:20 | 20210412–09:05 | 20210414–08:24 | 20210416–12:30 |

6 Test Results and Analysis

a) The statistics of domain name resolution results for Google public local DNS server 8.8.8.8 are shown in Table 4.

Table 4. Statistics of 8.8.8.8

Ns	Date											
Result	0326	0329	0331	0401	0402	0406	0407	0412	0414	0416	SUM	Successful rate
1A	8	4	2	4	3	0	6	5	7	3	42	42%
1AAAA	4	6	8	6	5	9	7	8	6	5	64	64%
2A	7	4	0	5	8	1	6	0	5	3	39	39%
2AAAA	6	6	1	6	3	0	3	4	5	9	43	43%
3A	3	2	8	4	6	7	6	6	1	6	49	49%
3AAAA	4	1	8	5	8	10	2	10	6	4	58	58%
4A1	5	8	2	1	1	1	5	0	7	3	33	100%
4A2	5	2	8	9	9	9	5	10	3	7	67	
4AAAA1	9	5	4	1	3	5	5	5	5	2	44	100%
4AAAA2	1	5	6	9	7	5	5	5	5	8	56	

DNS server IP:8.8.8.8

Ptr record:dns.google

Ptr domain name's A record:8.8.4.4 8.8.8.8

AAAA record:2001:4860:4860::8844 2001:4860:4860::8888

Type of LDNS server: cache server

Recursive server IP: according to the region where the client IP address is resolved, different recursive servers are used. Netease DNS tool is used to test three times on June 3, 2021. The recursive server addresses are 173.194.170.67 (Dutch IP), 74.125.114.198 (American IP) and 173.194.170.105 (Dutch IP) (note: the IP address territorial information is from www.ip138.com, the same below).

Summary: DNS Google is a DNS system with complete settings, providing IPv4 and IPv6 services at the same time, recursive servers distributed all over the world, and obtains resolution from IPv4 and IPv6 authorization servers at the same time.

b) The statistics of domain name resolution results for 114 public local DNS server 114.114.114.114 are shown in Table 5.

Table 5. Statistics of 114.114.114.114.

Ns	Date											
Result	0326	0329	0331	0401	0402	0406	0407	0412	0414	0416	Sum	Successful rate
1A	10	10	10	10	10	10	10	10	10	10	100	100%
1AAAA	0	0	0	0	0	0	0	0	0	0	0	0%
2A	10	10	10	10	10	10	10	10	10	10	100	100%
2AAAA	10	10	10	10	10	10	10	10	10	10	100	100%
3A	0	0	0	0	0	0	0	0	0	0	0	0%
3AAAA	0	0	0	0	0	0	0	0	0	0	0	0%
4A1	10	10	10	10	10	10	10	10	10	10	100	100%
4A2	0	0	0	0	0	0	0	0	0	0	0	
4AAAA1	10	10	10	10	10	10	10	10	10	10	100	100%
4AAAA2	0	0	0	0	0	0	0	0	0	0	0	

DNS server IP: 114.114.114.114
Ptr record: public1.114dns.com
Ptr domain name's A record: 114.114.114.114, no AAAA record.
Type of LDNS server: cache server
Recursive server IP: Netease DNS tool is used to test three times on June 3, 2021. The recursive server addresses are 58.217.249.155(NanJin Telcom IP), 219.148.204.132(ShengYang Telcom IP), 58.217.249.148(NanJin Telcom IP)
Summary: 114 DNS currently provides services for IPv4 (or dual stack) users, and only obtains the resolution from the IPv4 authorization server

c) The statistics of domain name resolution results for CERNET public local DNS server 202.38.184.13 are shown in Table 6.

Table 6. Statistics of 202.38.184.13

Ns	Date											
Result	0326	0329	0331	0401	0402	0406	0407	0412	0414	0416	Sum	Successful rate
1A	10	10	10	10	10	10	10	10	10	10	100	100%
1AAAA	0	0	0	0	0	0	0	0	0	0	0	0%
2A	10	10	10	10	10	10	10	10	10	10	100	100%
2AAAA	10	10	10	10	10	10	10	10	10	10	100	100%
3A	0	0	0	0	0	0	0	0	0	0	0	0%
3AAAA	0	0	0	0	0	0	0	0	0	0	0	0%
4A1	10	10	10	10	10	10	10	10	10	10	100	100%
4A2	0	0	0	0	0	0	0	0	0	0	0	
4AAAA1	10	10	10	10	10	10	10	10	10	10	100	100%
4AAAA2	0	0	0	0	0	0	0	0	0	0	0	

DNS server IP: 202.38.184.13
Ptr record: CS.NIC.EDU.CN
Ptr domain name's A record: 202.38.184.29 202.38.184.13, no AAAA record
202.38.184.13 can't resolve tools.netease.com, so the type of the DNS server remains to be checked.
Summary: CERNET DNS currently provides services for IPv4 (or dual stack) users, and only obtains the resolution from the IPv4 authorization server.

d) The statistics of domain name resolution results for Dalian Unicom public local DNS server 202.96.69.38 are shown in Table 7.

Table 7. Statistics of 202.96.69.38

Ns	Date											
Result	0326	0329	0331	0401	0402	0406	0407	0412	0414	0416	Sum	Successful rate
1A	8	0	0	0	0	0	0	0	0	2	10	10%
1AAAA	7	10	10	10	10	10	10	10	10	10	97	97%
2A	8	0	0	3	0	0	0	0	0	3	14	14%
2AAAA	7	0	0	0	0	0	0	0	0	0	7	7%
3A	7	10	7	2	10	10	10	10	9	10	85	85%
3AAAA	5	7	8	3	2	6	7	5	5	10	58	58%
4A1	7	5	7	0	3	4	6	5	4	0	41	100%
4A2	3	5	3	10	7	6	4	5	6	10	59	
4AAAA1	7	3	0	0	0	0	0	0	0	0	10	100%
4AAAA2	3	7	10	10	10	10	10	10	10	10	90	

DNS server IP: 202.96.69.38

Ptr record: dns.dl.lnpta.net.cn

Ptr domain name's A record: 202.96.69.38, no AAAA record

Type of LDNS server: cache server

Recursive server IP: Netease DNS tool is used to test three times on June 3, 2021. The recursive server addresses are 218.25.128.78, 218.25.128.74, 218.25.128.82(Dalian Unicom IP)

Summary: Dalian Unicom local DNS currently provides services for IPv4 (or dual stack) users, and obtains the DNS system for resolution from IPv4 and IPv6 authoritative servers. From the statistical data, it focuses more on obtaining resolution from IPv6 authorized servers.

e) The statistics of domain name resolution results for Dalian Mobile public local DNS server 211.137.32.178 are shown in Table 8.

Table 8. Statistics of 211.137.32.178

Ns	Date											
Result	0326	0329	0331	0401	0402	0406	0407	0412	0414	0416	Sum	Successful rate
1A	2	3	2	0	0	6	0	0	0	4	17	17%
1AAAA	4	10	10	8	7	10	7	10	5	8	79	79%
2A	4	7	2	3	3	7	3	2	3	5	39	39%
2AAAA	3	4	2	3	4	10	1	2	1	0	30	30%
3A	9	10	10	8	7	7	10	10	8	9	88	88%
3AAAA	9	8	9	10	9	7	10	10	10	9	91	91%
4A1	0	0	0	2	5	0	0	0	0	4	11	100%
4A2	10	10	10	8	5	10	10	10	10	6	89	
4AAAA1	4	0	3	2	0	6	0	0	0	2	17	100%
4AAAA2	6	10	7	8	10	4	10	10	10	8	83	

DNS server IP: 211.137.32.178

Ptr record: liaoning-chinamobile-dns.ln.chinamobile.com

Ptr domain name's A record: no A record, no AAAA records

Type of LDNS server: cache server

Recursive server IP: Netease DNS tool is used to test three times on June 3, 2021. The recursive server addresses are 221.180.132.153,221.180.132.152, 221.180.132.155(Dalian Mobile IP)

Summary: Dalian Mobile's local DNS currently provides services for IPv4 (or dual stack) users, and obtains the DNS system for resolution from IPv4 and IPv6 authoritative servers. From the statistical data, it focuses more on obtaining resolution from IPv6 authorized servers.

f) The statistics of domain name resolution results for Dalian Telcom public local DNS server 219.149.6.99 are shown in Table 9.

Table 9. Statistics of 219.149.6.99.

Ns	Date											
Result	0326	0329	0331	0401	0402	0406	0407	0412	0414	0416	Sum	Successful rate
1A	0	4	0	0	10	0	0	10	2	6	32	32%
1AAAA	10	0	5	10	10	10	2	6	10	10	73	73%
2A	10	5	0	10	0	0	6	10	10	0	51	51%
2AAAA	5	6	4	10	0	0	0	7	0	10	42	42%
3A	0	0	10	10	10	10	10	0	6	10	66	66%
3AAAA	5	10	5	10	0	4	0	10	4	10	58	58%
4A1	0	10	10	6	6	0	10	10	6	0	58	100%
4A2	10	0	0	4	4	10	0	0	4	10	42	
4AAAA1	5	3	4	10	5	4	0	5	0	4	40	100%
4AAAA2	5	7	6	0	5	6	10	5	10	6	60	

DNS server IP:219.149.6.99
Ptr record:dns2.lntele.com
Ptr domain name's A record: 219.149.6.99 no AAAA record
Type of LDNS server: cache server
Recursive server IP: Netease DNS tool is used to test three times on June 3, 2021. The recursive server addresses are 219.149.9.36,219.149.9.37(Dalian Telcom IP)
Summary: Dalian Telecom Local DNS currently provides services for IPv4 (or dual stack) users, and obtains the resolved DNS system from IPv4 and IPv6 authoritative servers.

7 Summary

Through the analysis of the test data of the above 6 common local DNS servers, the following conclusions can be drawn:

a) In terms of resolution acquisition methods, it is basically divided into two categories. The first, only obtains DNS resolution from the IPv4 authorization server. For example: 202.38.184.13 (CS.NIC.EDU.CN) and 114.114.114.114 (public1.114dns.com). In the second, the resolution records are obtained from IPv4 and IPv6 at the same time, but different weights will be used to return the obtained resolution to the user.

b) When the IPv6 authorized DNS server is set, both the A and AAAA records need to be published at the same time in the IPv4 and IPv6 authorized DNS servers, otherwise the resolution may fail.

c) With the implementation of Yeti DNS Testbed [6, 7] China has the root server of IPv6 DNS server, and the domain name resolution will be more guaranteed to be published to IPv6 DNS server. After the IPv4 domain name root server is blocked, the domain name can be resolved through IPv6 network.

d) Among the PTR domain names of the six public local DNS servers, only Google DNS has corresponding AAAA records. At present, the public local DNS server is mainly for IPv4 or dual stack clients. The pure IPv6 network is generally in universities and other research units, the public local DNS server is rarely used.

The resolution strategy of the local DNS server also changes with the transition from IPv4 to IPv6, and finally complete DNS resolution only through IPv6 network.

References

1. Paul Albitz, C.L.: DNS and BIND, 5th edn. O'Reilly, New York (2001)
2. Bao, C., Huitema, C., Bagnulo, M., Boucadair, M., Li, X.: Rfc6052: IPv6 Addressing of IPv4/IPv6 Translators. IETF (2010). www.rfc-editor.org/rfc/rfc6052.txt
3. Bagnulo, M., Matthews, P., vanBeijnum, I.: Rfc6146: Stateful NAT64: Network Address and Protocol Translation from IPv6 Clients to IPv4 Servers. IETF (2011). www.rfc-editor.org/rfc/rfc6146.txt
4. Li, X., Bao, C., Chen, M., Zhang, H., Wu, J.: Rfc6219: The China Education and Research Network (CERNET) IVI Translation Design and Deployment for the IPv4/IPv6 Coexistence and Transition. IETF (2011). www.rfc-editor.org/rfc/rfc6219.txt
5. Bagnulo, M., Sullivan, A., Matthews, P., van Beijnum, I.: Rfc6147: DNS64: DNS Extensions for Network Address Translation from IPv6 Clients to IPv4 Servers. IETF (2011). www.rfc-editor.org/rfc/rfc6147.txt
6. The next generation Internet root server experimental project "snowman plan" was officially released. China Education Network, Beijing (2015)
7. Song, L., Liu, D., Vixie, P., Kato, A., Kerr, S.: Rfc8483: Yeti DNS Testbed., IETF (2018). www.rfc-editor.org/rfc/rfc8483.txt

Experimental Evaluation of the Efficiency of Compression of Files by Fractal-Spectral Codec

Saida Beknazarova[1]([✉]), Nodira Muxtarjanovna Latipova[2],
Munira Jurayevna Maxmudova[2], and Viktoriya Sergeevna Alekseeva[2]

[1] Tashkent University of Information Technologies Named After Muhammad Al-Khwarizmi, Tashkent, Uzbekistan
saida.beknazarova@gmail.com
[2] National University of Uzbekistan Named After Mirzo Ulugbek, Tashkent, Uzbekistan

Abstract. In the article describe the estimation of the accuracy of image reconstruction by lifting filters, that in video codecs, the main compression of the video stream is provided by eliminating inter-frame redundancy using motion compensation methods for image fragments of adjacent frames. However, the use of motion compensation methods requires the formation of additional data (metadata) containing information about the types of image blocks used, the coordinates of their movement, etc. At the same time, in order to increase the compression of the video stream without compromising its quality, higher accuracy of motion compensation is required, which leads to an increase in the number of blocks and, accordingly, to an increase in the volume of metadata that reduces the effectiveness of motion compensation. This is the main problem of compressing streaming video without degrading the quality of images. In addition, the higher accuracy of positioning blocks with motion compensation dramatically reduces the speed of image processing, which is not always feasible in real-time system.

Keywords: Images · Metadata · Streaming video · Compression

1 Introduction

In the modern world, television, as a mass media, plays a very important role in the life of every person, because it allows you to convey information to him from almost any part of the world. At the same time, digital technologies are being actively introduced in the television industry. However, when converting an analog television signal into digital form, the output stream of video data can reach 240 Mbit/s [1, 2], which is 108 GB per hour of transmission. This requires a communication channel with a bandwidth of 120 MHz for their transmission and, accordingly, does not allow such a huge amount of information to be transmitted either over standard 8 MHz radio channels, or even more so over cellular communication channels with a bandwidth of 2 Mbit/s. In addition, the operations of recording and reproducing such large amounts of information on a personal computer are still fraught with serious difficulties. Therefore, to coordinate the parameters of signals and transmission channels, various methods of video compression are used, based on the elimination of redundant information of TV images. If they are not used, the average movie will take hundreds of gigabytes.

In this regard, one of the most urgent tasks in the field of audio-video data processing is the development and improvement of audio-video data compression methods, taking into account the elimination of temporary redundancy of TV images and audio accompaniment. This problem is very relevant in the conditions of the global financial crisis, in conditions of limited frequency resources. In addition, it becomes possible to significantly reduce the time for preparing television reports for broadcast directly from the event sites by transmitting signals from TV cameras directly to the installation hardware of television centers over cellular networks, and the need to use expensive and not always available broadband communication channels disappears.

Digital image processing is a rapidly developing field of science. Research and development of methods and algorithms for processing and analyzing information presented in the form of digital images is a very urgent task.

The great contribution to the digital processing of television images was made by both domestic scientists – V.T. Fisenko [3], M.L. Mestetsky [5], V.P. Dvorkovich, A.V. Dvorkovich [9], M.K. Chobanu [5], V.N. Kozlov [7], V.N. Gridin [8], V.Yu. Visilter [4], A.L. Priorov [9], as well as by L. Shapiro [7], R. Gonzalez [7], R. Woods [1], G. Finlayson [8], C. Wöhler [10], R. Szeliski [6], D. Maier [8].

The number of fundamental studies of B.A.Alpatov, O.I Atakishchev., O.E., Bashmakov, P.E Bykov., S.B. Gurevich, R.Duda, P. Hart and others are devoted to the development of methods for detecting and tracking moving objects, image processing and control of objects and purposeful processes. Methods of digital image processing were considered in the works of R.Gonzalez, A.A. Lukyanitsa, B.C. Titov, S.A. Filist Issues related to the transmission of video data were investigated in the works of Yu.B. Zubarev, Yu.S. Sogdulaev, etc. Methods of recognition of static and dynamic images based on spatio-temporal analysis of video images were covered in the works of M.N. Favorskaya, V.A. Soifer, V.T. Fisenko, D. Foresight, I.A. Klyuchikov, etc. At the same time, the issues of recognition of moving people (dynamic images) in various situations and in conditions of changing factors (interference, lighting heterogeneity, change of angle, etc.) remain unresolved.

The analysis of the literature has shown that the systems using algorithms of applied television are of the greatest interest. Such systems use the visible part of the electromagnetic spectrum, which is convenient for practical use [2, 3]. To date, applied television systems are widely used to perform various kinds of measurement work: diagnostics of the road network [1, 2]; detection of pedestrians [2]; detection of obstacles on the runway [2–6]; collision prevention on railways [2–8]; detection of obstacles in front of a mobile ground object [1–5]. All the listed systems using the methods of applied television to perform their task analyze a specific type of obstacle, without solving the problem in the general case. In this regard, a system of applied television based on digital image processing is proposed to solve the problem of detecting obstacles in the room by an autonomous mobile robotic platform, which characterizes in such an obstacle, the system is the main color feature, information, which makes it possible to distinguish the types of the underlying surface.

The purpose of the scientific article is to develop models, methods and algorithms for processing complex structured video data based on the use of methods to increase the contrast of television images in video information systems.

Frequency methods of image transformations are based on the idea of the Fourier transform, the meaning of which is to represent the original function as a sum of trigonometric functions of various frequencies multiplied by specified coefficients. An important property is that the function represented by the Fourier transform, after performing transformations on it, can be returned to its original form. This approach allows you to process the function in the frequency domain, and then return to the original form without loss of information. The Fourier transform can also be used to solve image filtering problems. In a practical application, the implementation of frequency approaches can be similar to spatial filtering methods.

Spatial image enhancement techniques are applied to raster images represented as two-dimensional matrices. The principle of spatial algorithms is to apply special operators to each point of the original image. Rectangular or square matrices called masks, kernels or windows act as operators. Most often, the mask is a small two-dimensional array, and improvement methods based on this approach are often called mask processing or mask filtering.

The existing methods of isolating (filtering) significant characteristics of individual image components, some periodic image structures are not optimal from the point of view of Fourier approximation in the specified frequency intervals in which filtering is carried out. Therefore, an urgent problem is the creation of mathematical models and filtering methods that allow for adequate consideration of the energy characteristics of images in selected frequency intervals. The paper develops and theoretically substantiates a method of optimal linear image filtering based on frequency representations, which is optimal in the sense that the spectrum of the image obtained as a result of filtering has the smallest standard deviation from the spectrum of the filtered image in a given two-dimensional frequency subinterval, and outside this subinterval has the smallest deviation from zero.

Usually, images are distorted under the influence of various kinds of interference. This complicates both their visual analysis by a specialist and automatic processing using computer technology. Attenuation of the interference effect can be achieved using various image filtering methods. When filtering, the brightness of each point of the source image distorted by interference is replaced by some other brightness value, which is assumed to be distorted to a lesser extent. Such a decision can be made based on the following considerations. The image is represented by a two-dimensional function of spatial coordinates, the values of which change more slowly when moving from point to point of the image than the values of a two-dimensional function describing interference. This allows, when evaluating the value of the useful signal at each point of the image, to take into account a certain set of neighboring points, taking advantage of a certain degree of similarity of the useful signal at these points.

Therefore, in video codecs, the main compression of the video stream is provided by eliminating inter-frame redundancy using motion compensation methods for image fragments of adjacent frames. However, the use of motion compensation methods requires the formation of additional data (metadata) containing information about the types of image blocks used, the coordinates of their movement, etc. At the same time, in order to increase the compression of the video stream without compromising its quality, higher accuracy of motion compensation is required, which leads to an increase in the number of blocks and, accordingly, to an increase in the volume of metadata that reduces the effectiveness of motion compensation. This is the main problem of compressing streaming video without degrading the quality of images. In addition, the higher accuracy of positioning blocks with motion compensation dramatically reduces the speed of image processing, which is not always feasible in real-time systems. Therefore, MPEG-4-10 codecs use a rectangular block structure of variable size, which provides acceptable image quality at speeds of more than 3 Mbit/s. Thus, the main problem of compressing a video stream without visually degrading the quality of images in real-time is the fairly large amount of metadata required to decode compressed images. To date, this problem has not yet been fully solved in world practice.

Additionally, the quality of images is indirectly affected by the amount of compression of audio signals, since both video and sound are transmitted in a single stream at a speed of 2 Mbit/s. At the same time, the volume of audio information, depending on the sound quality, can reach 10–20% of the video. Therefore, we must strive to increase the compression of audio signals. In this regard, the works aimed at improving the methods and algorithms of compression of streaming video and sound, to increase the compression coefficients without a noticeable decrease in the quality of the restored images and sound are of great scientific and practical importance.

2 Methodology

The analysis of the conducted studies showed that the best in image compression are VF LeGall (5,3), Deslauriers-Dubuc (9,7) and Deslauriers-Dubuc (13,7). But since all the filters considered use integer rounding of the division results, accordingly, with the reverse VP, some distortions of the restored video data occur. Therefore, to assess the accuracy of video data recovery by the considered VFS, a study of their effectiveness in processing 2 artificial and 2 real images presented in Figs. 1 and 2. The efficiency was evaluated based on the calculation of the root-mean-square error (RMS) of the original and reconstructed test images after processing by the LeGall (5,3), Deslauriers-Dubuc (9,7) and Deslauriers-Dubuc (13,7) VFS. According to the results of the experiments, it was found that monochrome images of the type of Fig. 1, and all the considered VFS are restored completely, without distortion.

As follows from the research results, the magnitude of the root-mean-square error of restoring test images is mainly determined by the structure of the image itself, and not by the type of the selected VF. Thus, the maximum error (2.9%) occurs when processing a fine-structured mountain landscape, images with a more homogeneous structure are restored with less distortion, and Deslauriers-Dubuc filters have the best quality characteristics Fig. 3. However, to build microprocessor video codecs, it is better to use LeGall

(5,3) filters, which have 2–3 times higher performance than Deslauriers-Dubuc filters, which allows using a cheaper and more accessible element base. And a small level of introduced distortion, not exceeding a few fractions of a percent, is not perceived by the human eye.

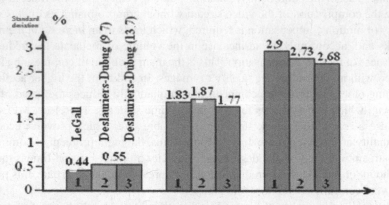

Fig. 1. Errors in the recovery of test images after processing.

The use of wavelet transformations, as well as DCP in codecs of standards (JPEG and MPEG) does not in itself reduce the volume of video data, but only allows them to be represented as chains of zero values of the coefficients of the decorated pixels. At the same time, video data compression is performed by statistical compressors by packing chains of coefficients with zero values. Thus, the more homogeneous the image was used, the longer the chains of zero coefficients are formed after the VP, and accordingly, a greater compression of the video data volume can be obtained. However, the problem with compression is that the amount of redundant information in an image strongly depends on its plot. Thus, Fig. 1 shows examples of compression of images of various subjects without loss of quality [1].

Therefore, quantization is used to control the amount of video data compression, in which the VP coefficients are divided into certain numbers, followed by rounding the result to integer values. This, on the one hand, reduces the dynamic range of coefficients, which require fewer data bits to be stored, and on the other hand, increases the length of zero coefficient chains, which increases the image data compression ratio. However, the structure of these VP coefficients is different than with PREP and represents nested quadrants. So Fig. 2 shows the original image and the result of a single VP. To date, an effective mechanism of inseparable VP has not yet been developed, so the transformation is carried out in 2 stages: first horizontally, then vertically. At the same time, 4 regions are formed: containing only low-frequency coefficients – low-frequency, only high–frequency coefficients – high-frequency and overlapping regions containing high-frequency and low-frequency coefficients (Fig. 2). With a larger number of transformations, only the low-frequency region (low-frequency) is processed, and the remaining regions remain unchanged.

Thus, in the quantizer, the coefficients of the quadrants are divided by a predetermined number, and each wavelet filter has its own coefficients [2].

Fig. 2. The initial image and the result of a single-level VP.

Most wavelet codecs use scalar quantization. There are two main strategies for performing scalar quantization. If the distribution of coefficients in each band is known in advance, then it is optimal to use Lloyd quantizers - with limited entropy for each subband [3]. In general, we do not have such knowledge, but we can transmit a parametric description of the coefficients by sending additional bits to the decoder. However, in practice, a simpler uniform quantizer with a "dead" zone is often used. Quantization intervals have size Δ, except for the central interval (near zero), whose size is usually chosen 2Δ (Fig. 3).

The value of the centroid of this interval is assigned to the coefficient that falls within a certain interval. In the case of asymptotically high coding rates, uniform quantization is optimal. Although in practical modes of operation, quantizers with a "dead" zone are suboptimal, they work almost as well as Lloy-da-Max quantizers, but are much simpler in execution [2]. In addition, they are resistant to changes in the distribution of coefficients in the subband. An additional advantage of them is that they can be nested into each other to obtain a nested bitstream [4].

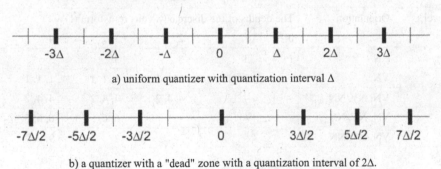

a) uniform quantizer with quantization interval Δ

b) a quantizer with a "dead" zone with a quantization interval of 2Δ.

Fig. 3. Variants of quantum converters with uniform and with a "dead" zone.

Below in tabular form (Table 1, 2 and 3) the default quantization coefficients for some wavelet filters are given depending on the depth of the VP, which in turn is also a variable number less than or equal to 4 [4].

Table 1. Values of the quantizer matrix for the Legal wavelet filter (5,3).

Level	Orientation	The depths of the discrete wavelet transform (DWT)				
		0	1	2	3	4
0	NN	0	4	4	4	4
1	VN	–	2, 2, 1	2, 2, 1	2, 2, 1	2, 2, 1
2	VN, NV, NN	–	–	4, 4, 2	4, 4, 2	4, 4, 2
3	VN, NV, NN	–	–	–	5, 5, 3	5, 5, 3
4	VN, NV, NN	–	–	–	–	7, 7, 5

Table 2. Values of the quantizer matrix for the wavelet filter Deslauriers-Dubuc (13,7).

Level	Orientation	The depths of the discrete wavelet transform (DWT)				
		0	1	2	3	4
0	NN	1	5	5	5	5
1	VN	–	3, 3, 1	3, 3, 1	3, 3, 1	3, 3, 1
2	VN, NV, NN	–	–	4, 4, 1	4, 4, 1	4, 4, 1
3	VN, NV, NN	–	–	–	5, 5, 2	5, 5, 2
4	VN, NV, NN	–	–	–	–	6, 6, 3

Table 3. Values of the quantizer matrix for the wavelet filter Daubechies (9,7).

Level	Orientation	The depths of the discrete wavelet transform (DWT)				
		0	1	2	3	4
0	NN	1	3	3	3	3
1	VN	–	1, 1, 1	1, 1, 1	1, 1, 1	1, 1, 1
2	VN, NV, NN	–	–	4, 4, 2	4, 4, 2	4, 4, 2
3	VN, NV, NN	–	–	–	6, 6, 5	6, 6, 5
4	VN, NV, NN	–	–	–	–	9, 9, 7

3   Discussion

By varying these numbers for different conversion levels and different quadrants, you can control the degree of video data loss in the image, thereby changing the compression ratio and the quality of the restored images. At the same time, to ensure the constancy of the bitrate of the compressed video stream, an adaptive change in the values of the quantization coefficients is used, which maintains the constancy of the frame compression ratio when excessive information changes in them. At the same time, the quantization coefficients calculated in the compressor are stored in the output array for proper operation of the decompressor. However, an increase in video data compression leads to an increase in irreversible data loss, which affects the visual quality of the restored images. Therefore, determining the optimal values of the quantizer is a rather difficult task and requires further research.

One of the most urgent tasks in the field of audio-video data processing is the improvement of audio-video data compression methods, taking into account the elimination of temporary redundancy of TV images and audio accompaniment. This problem is very relevant in conditions of limited frequency resources. In addition, it becomes possible to significantly reduce the preparation time for television reports to be broadcast directly from the event sites by transmitting signals from TV cameras directly to the installation hardware of television centers over cellular networks. At the same time, there is no need to use expensive and not always available broadband communication channels.

As a result of the conducted research, TV images have code, intra-frame statistical, psychovisual, structural, temporal, or inter-frame redundancy, when eliminated, image information reduction or video data compression is achieved.

Statistical redundancy is eliminated by the use of spectral transformations based on PREP and VP and allows you to compress images by 20–20 times for PREP and 30–40 for VP, and with virtually no data loss.

The presence of psych visual redundancy allows you to control the codec compression ratio by removing that part of useful information that is either not perceived by our visual system or makes it little noticeable. This approach makes it possible to increase codec compression and, while maintaining visual quality, image compression can be obtained up to 40 times with PREP and 60–70 times with VP. However, with high compression ratios, there are noticeable image distortions in the form of a block structure in PREP or a loss of clarity in VP.

The presence of inter-frame redundancy makes it possible to further increase the compression of the video stream to about 80–90 times due to the use of various motion compensation methods. However, these methods for the correct recovery of images during decoding form an additional array of metadata carrying information, but new coordinates of the moved blocks, pointers of block types, etc. Metadata is added to the compressed image data in a single digital stream and must be protected from possible errors, otherwise, it will not be possible to restore the image. Moreover, to ensure a higher compression ratio, a more accurate operation of the motion compensator is required by reducing the size of the blocks, changing their geometry, or adapting their shape to the configuration of the video objects of the scene (adaptive compensation). However, this leads to a significant increase in the volume of metadata, and accordingly to a decrease in the resulting compression ratio of the video stream, negating all the advantages of motion compensation. Therefore, increased compression can only be achieved by degrading the quality of the images.

Fractal compression methods based on the elimination of structural redundancy can provide the required compression of the video stream by 150–200 times, but they have very low performance and currently cannot provide real-time processing of the video stream [16].

Thus, to date, existing image processing algorithms can only achieve 130–150 times compression of the video stream due to a noticeable deterioration in their visual quality. Therefore, to ensure good quality of TV images with a frame size of 8–10 kBytes, it is necessary to develop new effective methods for processing video streams that significantly minimize the amount of metadata (no more than 500 bytes per frame), or do not use motion compensation at all.

4   Conclusion

Experimental evaluation of the efficiency of compression of audio files by fractal and fractal-spectral codec. To evaluate the effectiveness of the proposed method of audio signal compression based on the elimination of temporary redundancy of audio frames, an experimental study of the compression of audio files of various genres with various errors in the identification of audio frames was conducted.

Currently, Haar wavelets are widely used for information compression, which is characterized by simplicity of implementation, since it has only 2 coefficients. However, the Haar wavelet is not very suitable for compressing audio signals, because it does not provide a high degree of compression of the ZS, since when a large number of conversion coefficients are discarded, distortions occur in the form of extraneous noise, crackling and rumbling. To eliminate this disadvantage, higher-order wavelets can be used, for example, Daubeshi-4th order, having 4 coefficients and Daubeshi-10, having 10 coefficients [4, 14]. Moreover, the functions of higher-order wavelets have a more "smooth" shape, due to which the compression ratio can be increased while maintaining the sound quality. Therefore, for the implementation of the compression algorithm, it is most advisable to use the Dobshy wavelet of the 10th order, since on the one hand, it provides greater conversion accuracy, and on the other, it does not significantly reduce the processing speed.

References

1. Artyushenk, V.M., Shelukhin, O.I., Afonin, M.Y.: Digital Compression of Video Information and Sound, p. 430. Moscow (2003)
2. Vatolin, D., Ratushnyak, A., Smirnov, M., Yukin, V.: Data compression methods. http://com pression.graphicon.ru/
3. Salomon, D.: Data, Image and Sound Compression. Technosphere, Moscow (2004)
4. Vorobyov, V.I., Gribunin, V.G.: Theory and Practice of the Wavelet Transform. VUS, St. Petersburg (1999)
5. Boriskevich, A.A.: Electronic Educational and Methodological Complex on the Discipline "Digital Speech and Image Processing", 124 p. Minsk (2007)
6. Onthriar, K., Loo, K.K., Xue, Z.: Performance Comparison of Emerging Dirac Video Codec with H.264/AVC. In: International Conference on Digital Telecommunication (ICDT'06) (2006)
7. Salomon, D.: Data Compression. Springer, New York (2007)
8. Sayood, K.: Introduction to Data Compression. Wiley-Interscience, New York (2006)
9. Krintz, C., Sucu, S.: Adaptive on-the-fly compression. IEEE Trans. Parallel Distrib. Syst. 17, 15–24 (2006)

10. Pan, Y., Guo, X., Lin, H., Luo, S.: Proceedings of 2020 ACM International Conference Proceeding Series, pp. 130–133 (2020)
11. Lomtev, E.A., Myasnikova, M.G., Myasnikova, N.V., Tsypin, B.V.: Improvement of signal compression-restoration algorithms for remote measurement systems. Meas. Tech. **58**, 250–255 (2015)
12. Beknazarova, S., Bazhenov, R., Zatonskiy, A.: Advantages of freeware-based simulation tools for technical and technological modeling. In: Conference: 2021 International Conference on Industrial Engineering, Applications and Manufacturing (2021)
13. Cappello, F., et al.: Use cases of lossy compression for floating-point data in scientific data sets. Int. J. High Perform. Comput. Appl. **33**, 1201–1220 (2019)
14. Tao, D., Di, S., Chen, Z., Cappello, F.: IEEE International Parallel and Distributed Processing Symposium, pp. 1129–1139. IEEE, Orlando (2017)

An Intelligent Decision Support System for Solving Complex Territorial Planning Problems

Dmitry Gura[1]([✉]), Roman Dyachenko[1], Nafset Khusht[1], Jean Doumit[2], Daniil Drazhetsky[1], and Alexander Solodunov[1,3]

[1] Kuban State Technological University, 2, Moskovskaya Street, 350072 Krasnodar, Russian Federation
gurada@kubstu.ru
[2] Faculty of Letters and Human Sciences Branch 2, Geospatial Lab, Lebanese University, Beirut, Lebanon
[3] Kuban State Agrarian University, 13, Kalinina Street, 350044 Krasnodar, Russian Federation

Abstract. Territorial planning, which determines the prospects for the development of territories, can use laser scanning methods as a method for obtaining geospatial information about the territory. Currently, the data obtained by laser scanning is often processed manually by specialists. In the future, it is expedient to process large volumes of data using computer decision support systems, i.e. such computer systems that should help the decision maker in difficult conditions. These systems will be based on artificial intelligence methods for maximum efficiency, complete and objective data analysis. During processing, the computer system will have to analyze the incoming data, clean it up, select and classify objects, and assign semantic data. To do this, the system will have to go through the machine learning stage based on the training set. The problem of making optimal decisions is relevant, as it depends on many factors, and making the "right decision" means choosing the optimal one from a variety of options. The article provides an overview of the main definitions and terms in the field of decision making, and laser scanning techniques. The novelty is the proposal to use a decision support system for processing data obtained using laser scanning and application for the engineering direction of territorial planning.

Keywords: DSS · Expert system · Territorial planning · Laser scanning · 3D-model · Artificial intelligence · Machine learning · Big data · SDGs

1 Introduction

At the moment, the increase in urban areas is moving at a very fast pace. The development of a modern city cannot do without methods of territorial planning. In the Town Planning Code of the Russian Federation, territorial planning is understood as the determination of the purpose of the territory for the purposes of sustainable development of territories, the development of engineering, transport and social infrastructures, taking into account

A. Gibadullin (Ed.): ITIDMS 2021, CCIS 1703, pp. 22–31, 2022.
https://doi.org/10.1007/978-3-031-21340-3_3

the interests of the population and is considered as an analogue of the terms "Spatial planning" and "Regional planning" Territorial planning, as an element urban planning activities in the regulatory documentation defines as the main documents – territorial planning schemes, the preparation of which is carried out on the basis of the results of engineering surveys [1].

Modern technologies over the past decades have changed the approach to territorial planning towards the use of intelligent systems for the integrated, sustainable development of territories. When developing urban planning documentation, it is necessary to take into account the format and structure of the data received. As a replacement for the usual 2D data formats, 3D models are coming. The creation of a full-fledged cartographic basis for territorial planning schemes also cannot do without modern technologies, in particular, the use of laser scanning technology [2].

The processing of data obtained using laser scanning is a very important process, the automation of which is an urgent problem. As a solution to this problem, the use of an intelligent decision support system (IDSS) is proposed.

2 Materials and Methods

The problem of decision making has long been a priority area for research. Scientists from various fields of science have contributed to understanding how decision-making occurs in society, government, economics, industry and other important human activities. The task of decision making is the formation of a set of possible options that provide a solution to the problem under existing restrictions. The decision problem X can be represented as formula 1 [3].

$$X = \langle Y, Z \rangle \tag{1}$$

where Y is the set of solutions, Z is the principle of optimality.

The "right decision" is an alternative solution out of many possible ones, in which, taking into account various factors, the overall value will be optimized. By increasing the number of participants in the decision-making process using the latest technology, "accuracy" can be increased. The selection of one parameter that most fully and accurately characterizes the object, allows you to give it unconditional preference [3–5].

Decision support technologies include: expert systems (ES), decision support systems (DSS) and collective intelligence (CI) [4–6, 20].

The main source of knowledge when making a decision in such systems is an expert, i.e. bangs having knowledge in a particular subject area. The purpose of creating these systems is to form such a knowledge base that will contain the knowledge of a large number of experts. The standard composition of the EC is shown in Fig. 1.

As part of the ES, it is customary to single out the information and software parts, each of which includes certain blocks. The information part includes Database and Knowledge base. In the program part, it is customary to allocate blocks: Inference block; Decision explanation block – provides analysis and reasoning of decisions; Block of knowledge acquisition – needed to support the Knowledge engineer. Ensuring interaction with the system is provided using the interface.

A decision support system (DSS) is a computer system (CS) designed to help a decision maker (DM) in difficult conditions with the help of a complete and objective analysis. Such systems have emerged as a result of the combination of management information systems and database management systems (DBMS).

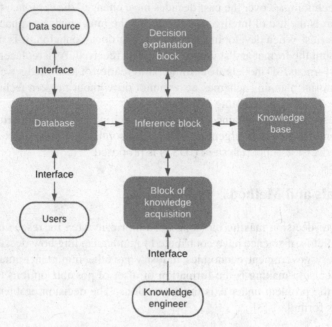

Fig. 1. The composition of the expert system.

The development of recommendations for the decision maker is based on the system's reasoning based on input data using various processing modules. The general scheme of the structure of the DSS is shown in Fig. 2.

The standard structure of the DSS includes an input data processing module, which is used to convert data into a format understandable for the program; DSS operation module is used for further transfer of incoming data to handler modules; modules handlers that implement the tasks of forecasting and inference. Handler modules include Fuzzy inference module, Scope module and Modeling module.

Fuzzy inference module is the main handler module. It serves to receive recommendations. Based on the received data and the fuzzy interpretation mechanism, the module issues the necessary recommendations. Scope module is used for database analysis. Analyzing the database, finds data related to each other, and issues recommendations. Modeling module required for issuing predictions based on user data.

The recommendation module is required by the CS to collect the results of the work of all handler modules and then issue them to the user through the interface, in the form of a window with recommendations.

Basically, the following main components are distinguished in the structure of the decision-making system:

Knowledge management system;
Model management system
User interface;
User (specialist).

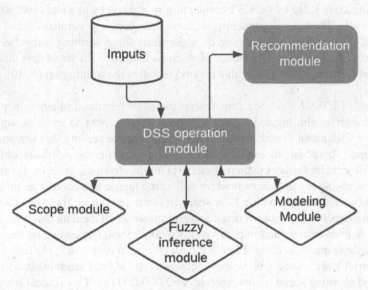

Fig. 2. DSS scheme.

As the main methods of work, the DSS can use: data mining, knowledge search in the database, information retrieval, simulation, neural networks, etc. [6].

One of the varieties of DSS is an intelligent decision support system (IDSS) – this is a decision support system based on artificial intelligence (AI) methods. Currently, many IDSS are based on expert systems that process knowledge and simulate the behavior of decision makers using certain rules of logic. Undoubtedly, the main source of knowledge in ES is an expert, and in certain situations (when the decision-making parameters are well known), ES show a better result than the original experts. The effectiveness of ES can also fall when new, yet unexplored and uncertain circumstances appear. Modern research in the field of AI has made it possible to introduce a number of methods necessary for ES to work more efficiently with new circumstances. These include knowledge sharing, machine learning, data mining, and automatic inference [7, 8].

IDSS by collecting and analyzing data, detecting and diagnosing problems, and suggesting and evaluating various options for action should function as a consultant – to support decision makers. With the help of AI methods built into IDSS, such a CS should imitate human capabilities as accurately as possible. CS training can be divided into the following main types:

- Obtaining data and knowledge by the COP, by direct input, without applying logical conclusions (mechanical memorization). The information is used in the form in which it was received by the CS.
- Obtaining CS data and knowledge from outside. External information goes through a system of transformations into formats that are convenient for using the CS and are used in the process of inference.
- Obtaining knowledge by the CS by collecting individual factors and processing them (meta-level). The CS independently acquires knowledge, generalizes it and systematizes it. This type of CS learning on algorithms for describing and reflecting the properties of an object is the essence of machine learning. The set of data that formed the basis for training the CS by this method is called the training set [9, 10].

The use of IDSS for solving complex problems of territorial planning is primarily associated with monitoring and control of current development, in terms of supervising compliance with urban planning regulations. Large remote sensing data obtained using laser scanning should be processed by IDSS in order to recognize individual objects and classes of objects for further creation of their 3D models from the processed point cloud.

Laser scanning is a unique method for collecting metric and coordinate information about an object. Shooting with a laser scanner is carried out at high speed and is the most accurate method in terms of detail and completeness of the data obtained, it allows you to work even at night and in poor visibility conditions. Depending on the shooting method, laser scanning is divided into 3 types (ground, mobile, air) [11, 12].

Terrestrial laser scanning is the most accurate type of laser scanning due to its high density and shooting speed (it can reach up to 2,000,000 t/s). This is ideal for shooting single subjects. It is suitable both for indoor shooting and for obtaining very detailed 3D models of objects, facade plans, etc. An important feature of terrestrial laser scanning is the need to use a geodetic base – points (marks) to which you can bind [12].

A feature of data acquisition during mobile laser scanning is the performance of shooting from a moving land or water carrier, usually in continuous mode. This system allows you to evenly remove any objects that fall into the field of view of the scanner. This type of scanning is suitable for shooting extended objects (for example, a road) [13].

Aerial laser scanning can be carried out both from manned aircraft and from unmanned aerial vehicles (UAVs). The result is a volumetric point cloud of a vast territory. Airborne laser scanning is mainly used to create a digital terrain model. It can also be used for various types of monitoring (for example, tracking land use in accordance with their intended purpose). Allows you to significantly reduce the time of work in comparison with standard methods of shooting objects. An important advantage is the ability to shoot in hard-to-reach areas (for example, in mountainous areas) [14].

The result of laser scanning is a large data array (three-dimensional point cloud of laser reflection). At the moment, the processing of data obtained using laser scanning occurs in a semi-automatic mode using specialized software and consists of the following steps: data preprocessing, vectorization and creation of a 3D model. Laser scanning allows you to create digital terrain models and 3D models of objects. Laser scanning data can be used to create topographic plans and maps, as well as longitudinal and transverse profiles [14], [15, 16].

The most efficient work of IDSS for laser scanning data processing will be carried out if the CS will be based on machine learning algorithms based on the generated training set and functioning according to the "training with a teacher" type.

For such systems, the teacher can be a person, the environment, or even the artificial system itself. The task of learning is to search for and identify patterns (certain dependencies) that combine data. In its simplest form, CS training can consist of 2 components (Fig. 3) [10].

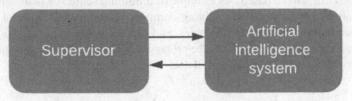

Fig. 3. IDSS training system.

Supervised learning assumes that the CS receives examples consisting of "known input – known output" pairs. The values obtained by the system at the output are compared with previously known values. In this case, the error of the results obtained by the system is calculated, on the basis of which a correction is made according to a certain algorithm. Extraction of CS knowledge from data in the form of dependencies and rules can be described by a single technique based on Data Mining methods [9, 17].

Acquisition of knowledge usually consists of the following steps:

- Obtaining initial data. At this stage, the active participation of the expert is necessary, since models will be built on their basis.
- Cleaning. A preliminary return is necessary, since the original data rarely turn out to be of high quality. Cleaning includes smoothing, gap filling, etc.
- Data transformation. The cleaned data set must be converted to a specific format and agreed upon. Required to maintain relationships between data and analyze them.
- Interpretation. Viewing and assigning values to data to draw certain conclusions.

The procedure for obtaining knowledge from laser scanning data for the purpose of applying them in territorial planning is shown in Fig. 4.

The introduction of AI into the processing of laser reflection point clouds has great advantages over the traditional method. They consist not only in simplifying and accelerating the processing process, but also in the ability of the system to "finish" the missing data, based on previously obtained knowledge [18].

3   Results

As a result of the analysis, algorithms were proposed for the full-fledged functioning of IDSS for processing geospatial data obtained using 3D laser scanning technologies as part of solving territorial planning problems.

As a working basis for IDSS, it is necessary to form a database that will contain information about the results of laser scanning of territories; choose the optimal database management system; choose the best methods and algorithms for data processing and analysis. These elements are necessary for the implementation of AI machine learning, on which the DSS will be based. An example of a training sequence is shown in Fig. 5.

The analysis shows that when solving complex problems of territorial planning, the use of modern information technologies, and especially the use of decision support technology, is economically justified. The proposed DSS will simplify and speed up the process of working with information and data.

4   Discussion

For a better study and understanding of the methodology for applying and creating a DSS, it is necessary to analyze other approaches to their design, in addition to the above method of applying and creating a DSS for territorial planning based on machine learning algorithms.

A similar decision to use DSS in territorial planning was made by the author of [19]. The main difference is that this work proposes the creation of a DSS for modeling the development of a city's infrastructure using a multi-agent approach.

The paper [20] describes the use of AI for territorial planning.

As another example, it is worth citing the work [21], which proposes the creation of a DSS to assess territorial sustainability. The use of multicriteria decision analysis by the system is described.

At the moment, most of the existing DSS are focused on solving a small number of tasks. At the same time, the experience of implementing ES to solve problems in a highly specialized area, although it shows their success, but the change in external factors affecting competitiveness and sustainability, shows that the more complex the organization becomes, the fewer decisions fall on decision makers or ES. For an important task, the organization is likely to reach out and prioritize a group of experts. To solve this problem, the experience of group decision making is used, which formed the basis of the group decision support system technology (GDSMS) [22, 23].

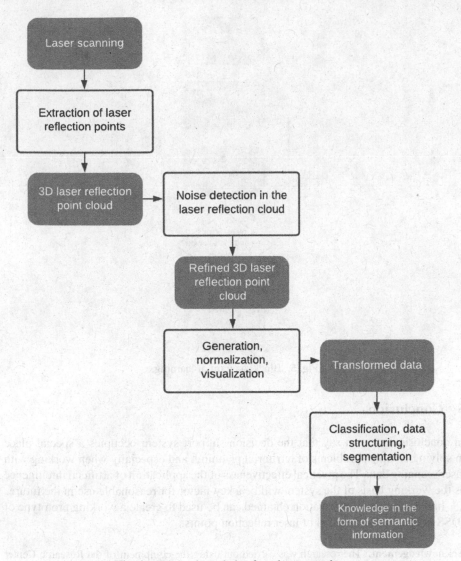

Fig. 4. Gaining knowledge from laser scan data.

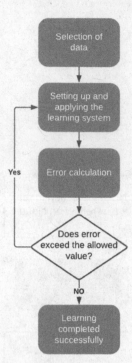

Fig. 5. Block diagram of learning.

5 Conclusion

In conclusion, we can say that the decision support system occupies a special place in solving complex problems of territorial planning, and especially when working with laser scanning data. The practical effectiveness of the application of artificial intelligence as the working basis of the system will be a key factor for reasonable use in the future.

In the future, the information obtained can be used to create a working prototype of IDSS for processing a cloud of laser reflection points.

Acknowledgement. The research was carried out using the equipment of the Research Center for Food and Chemical Technologies of KubSTU (CKP_3111) which development is supported by the Ministry of Science and Higher Education of the Russian Federation (Agreement No. 075-15-2021-679).

The research was carried out at the expense of the grant of the Russian Science Foundation No. 22-29-00849 "Development of an intelligent information system for decision-making support for solving complex problems of territorial planning using strong artificial intelligence".

References

1. Wang, Y., Sun, Y., Liu, Z., Sarma, S.E., Bronstein, M.M., Solomon, J.M.: Dynamic graph CNN for learning on point clouds. ACM Trans. Graphics (TOG) **38**(5), 1–12 (2019)
2. Te, G., Hu, W., Zheng, A., Guo, Z.: RGCNN: Regularized graph CNN for point cloud segmentation. In: Proceedings of the 26th ACM International Conference Multimedia, pp. 746–754 (2018)
3. Xu, Y., Fan, T., Xu, M., Zeng, L., Qiao, Y.: SpiderCNN: deep learning on point sets with parameterized convolutional filters. In: Ferrari, V., Hebert, M., Sminchisescu, C., Weiss, Y. (eds.) ECCV 2018. LNCS, vol. 11212, pp. 90–105. Springer, Cham (2018). https://doi.org/10.1007/978-3-030-01237-3_6
4. Komarichev, A., Zhong, Z., Hua, J.: A-CNN: Annularly convolutional neural networks on point clouds. In: Proceedings IEEE Conference Computer Vision Pattern Recognition (CVPR), pp. 7421–7430 (2019)
5. Qi, C.R., Yi, L., Su, H., Guibas, L.J.: PointNet++: Deep hierarchical feature learning on point sets in a metric space. In: Proceedings Advance Neural Information Processing System 30 (NIPS), pp. 5105–5114 (2017)
6. Ye, X., Li, J., Huang, H., Du, L., Zhang, X.: 3D recurrent neural networks with context fusion for point cloud semantic segmentation. In: Ferrari, V., Hebert, M., Sminchisescu, C., Weiss, Y. (eds.) ECCV 2018. LNCS, vol. 11211, pp. 415–430. Springer, Cham (2018). https://doi.org/10.1007/978-3-030-01234-2_25
7. Li, Y., Bu, R., Sun, M., Wu, W., Di, X., Chen, B.: PointCNN: Convolution On X-transformed points. In: Proceedings Advance Neural Information Process. System (NIPS), pp. 828–838 (2018)
8. Li, J., Chen, B.M., Lee, G.H.: SO-net: self-organizing network for point cloud analysis. In: Proceedings IEEE Conference Computer Vision Pattern Recognition (CVPR), pp. 9397–9406 (2018). https://doi.org/10.1109/cvpr.2018.00979
9. Su, H., Maji, S., Kalogerakis, E., Learned-Miller, E.: Multi-view convolutional neural networks for 3D shape recognition. In: Proceedings IEEE International Conference Computer Vision (ICCV), pp. 945–953 (2015)
10. Boulch, A., Le Saux, B., Audebert, N.: Unstructured point cloud semantic labeling using deep segmentation networks. In: Proceedings Eurograph. Workshop 3D Object Retreival, vol. 2, pp. 17–24 (2017)
11. Tchapmi, L., Choy, C., Armeni, I., Gwak, J., Savarese, S.: SEGCloud: Semantic segmentation of 3D point clouds. In: Proceedings Internatinal Conference 3D Vision (3DV), pp. 537–547 (2017)
12. Le T., Duan Y.: PointGrid: a deep network for 3D shape understanding. In: Proceedings IEEE Conference Computer Vision Pattern Recognition (CVPR), pp. 9204–9214 (2018)
13. Dyachenko, R., Gura, D., Samarin, S., Bespyatchuk, D., Solodunov, A.: Analysis of algorithms for terrestrial recognition of woody vegetation using 3D-laser scanning technology. In: IOP Conference Series: Earth and Environmental Science, vol. 867, issue 1 (2021)
14. Gura, D., Dubenko, Y., Markovskiy, I., Pshidatok, S.: Monitoring infrastructure facilities of territories in agricultural sector. In: IOP Conference Series: Earth and Environmental Science, 403 (2019)

Fault Tolerance of Distributed Worker Processes in Corporate Information Systems and Technologies

Teymur Zeynally$^{(\boxtimes)}$ ⓘ and Dmitry Demidov ⓘ

Moscow Polytechnic University, Moscow, Russian Federation
z.teymur.e@gmail.com, d.g.demidov@mospolytech.ru

Abstract. This paper proposes algorithms and methods for ensuring the fault tolerance of peer-to-peer worker processes in corporate information systems and technologies. The paper defines the concept of worker processes and the situations in which they are used in information technologies. Also, the current solutions are considered, the problems of ensuring fault tolerance are analyzed. The implementation and specifics of the proposed algorithms are based on the use of distributed blockers and key-value storages in information systems and technologies. Features of using distributed blockers, specifics of the coordination of the execution and the existing methods of implementation are described. The issues of service configuration and node prioritization are discussed. Results of the work are summed up and conclusions are drawn.

Keywords: Distributed system · Worker process · Distributed blocker · Key-value storage · Fault tolerance · Information systems · Information technologies

1 Introduction

At the moment, information systems of large companies require more and more computing resources for their functioning. In addition, there are high requirements for system fault tolerance and uptime. In such conditions, it is not enough just to increase the capacity of a single server and monitor its hardware, since this does not guarantee the fulfillment of the requirements and is only suitable for small enterprises. To ensure high reliability and guaranteed data processing time, information systems are scaled horizontally by adding new servers. If one node fails, or the communication channel with one data center is broken, then the rest of the system will continue to process traffic. The reliability and performance of distributed systems is directly proportional to the number of computers in the system [1].

A worker process is an iterative process applied to a wide range of tasks. A process is a set of actions performed within a single iteration. Worker processes are hosted by Windows services or UNIX daemons. They may include several parallel worker processes. The parallelism of the execution of worker processes is provided by the operating system threads. Worker processes are used to solve problems where iterative actions are needed in the system. For example, worker processes are used to process messages from a queue, perform individual steps of a large business scenario, send notifications, build reports, create backups, etc. Worker processes, as a rule, have a schedule according to which they are executed.

Depending on the type of schedule, the following types of worker processes can be distinguished:

- Recurrent worker – runs after a certain time interval. The time interval does not depend on the duration of one iteration.
- Cron worker – runs according to the crontab schedule.
- Workload worker is the most complex of all. The iteration execution time interval is described by a certain time range. The next iteration time depends on how much work has been done in the current iteration. As a general rule, the more work, the shorter the interval. The schedule involves setting the function for calculating the interval time. In some cases, breakpoints are provided for workload values.

Depending on the type of the execution, worker processes can be divided into:

- Sequential – a new iteration will not start until the previous one is completed.
- Parallel – each iteration is strictly on schedule.

2   Materials and Methods

The methodological basis of the current research is the analysis of algorithms and methods of worker processes functioning in corporate information systems and existing software packages. Current research also analyzes common problems in this area. As a result of the analysis, algorithms and methods for coordinating distributed worker processes without leader are proposed.

3   Results

3.1   Review of Existing Solutions

The most common solution in the dotnet area is Quartz, but it does not have the functionality to create the most important type of worker – the workload worker. The workload worker is used to dynamically adapt the system to an increasing load, and is most common on tasks that process message flows from queues. Quartz implements persistence through relational stores that can be interacted with through ADO.NET. Fault tolerance is provided by monitoring the states of nodes in storages. The current work will present a different approach to ensure fault tolerance using distributed blockers or key-value stores [4]. Distributed blockers use a different approach to organizing data, require fewer computing resources, and are easier to maintain, operate, and replicate [3].

The second solution for prevalence is Hangfire. It is not a completely free solution, just like Quartz does not support the workload worker [11]. Persistence is present, moreover, Hangfire does not work without a database [12]. But unlike Quartz, in the documentation, in addition to relational DBMS, there are NoSql storages for a paid subscription. However, the methods of working with key-value stores in Hangfire differ from those described in this paper.

There are also various kinds of simple solutions that can iteratively run code blocks on a schedule. For example, FluentScheduler is such a solution [13]. Supports only recurrent and cron worker, no persistence, failover, etc.

3.2 Fault Tolerance Problem

At first glance, it is not so difficult to ensure the fault tolerance of a service worker – another such service is required in a nearby data center.

In most cases, when, for example, messages from a queue are processed, distribution across data centers will only increase the speed of processing messages from the queue and the performance of the system as a whole. This applies well to independent serial or any parallel worker processes.

However, when distributed among data centers, the problem of coordinating iterations of worker processes arises. This problem arises due to in corporate information systems, for implementing the functionality of processing the stages of business scenarios, preference is given to sequential worker processes. This is due to the fact that the trigger for processing is a certain status of a tuple in a relational DBMS. And many systems are organized in such a way that the worker process processes data on the corresponding status of the tuple and transfers it to the next status, to trigger the next handler.

For example, consider a scenario for changing order parameters, consisting of the following steps: approval by a manager, changing order parameters, calling the delivery service API, sending SMS to the user. The example is simplified, but as a rule, each of the stages consists of fairly complex logic. And in corporate systems for this scenario, a tuple is assumed in the database table, with the "Status" attribute, which is processed in turn by 4 worker processes, transferring to the next status.

This code organization is called "workflow" and allows you to divide the process into stages independent of each other, which has a positive effect on the complexity of supporting such systems [14]. If the process is delayed, then the parallel execution of the same iteration is unacceptable. A parallel iteration will do the same thing as a delayed iteration. And to solve this problem, engineers begin to make a number of decisions that only exacerbate the situation. For example, a bad decision is to "take in processing" a tuple. The tuple is marked with the status "in processing" (for example, "sending SMS") and these tuples are ignored by parallel (or distributed) worker processes. However, if the process that took the worker into processing fails at the host or operating system level, then the tuple will forever remain in the "processing" status. Moreover, in cases where there are more than or equal to two nodes in the cluster, then the situation of the struggle for tuples in the DBMS is not uncommon. The struggle lies in the fact that each individual node of the cluster tries to take a lock in the database for a number of tuples, the other node, usually processing, tries to update the data in the neighboring tuple. Thus, in the DBMS, deadlocks begin on the sql pages, leading to degradation of the performance of the entire system. If a processing process becomes a victim of deadlock, then such a process simply cannot save the results of its work [2]. The situation is exacerbated in cases where processing occurs in a non-transactional system, and the handler itself is not idempotent. For example: sending emails, updating data via API in an external system, etc. Reprocessing in such cases is a violation of the requirements.

In cases where it is necessary to ensure the fault tolerance of a legacy project. Redesigning all processes to support parallel iterations is often too expensive (financially).

3.3 Usage of Distributed Blockers and Key-Value Storages

One relatively cheap solution is to use a distributed blocker. Adding a distributed blocker to a project brings with it an impressive number of problems, and in relation to worker processes, it is necessary to consider the specifics of these.

Developers of distributed blockers are aware of the difficulties with choosing a lock owner and provide certain functionality to control locks. They also know how to deal with failures of their own nodes. But in doing so, the application must adhere to a number of rules so as not to block the entire system forever or there are no situations where several nodes think they are holding the lock.

Distributed blockers are key-value stores and distributed blocker operations are atomic comparison with replacement. This means that in order to change a value by key, its current value must be passed [6]. This approach is often used in storage and is called "optimistic locking". Optimistic locking prevents collisions and maintains key integrity. In addition, the keys are equipped with a TTL (time to live) [6]. This is necessary to release the lock in the event that the node that took the lock has failed. The node can be equipped with a timer that will update the lock TTL while the process is running. It is necessary to choose the timings correctly in order to level the loss of TTL blocking due to network lags. But if, nevertheless, there was a failure in communication between the distributed blocker and the application, then in this case it is necessary to provide a watchdog timer that will abruptly stop the running thread, which obviously lost the lock. It is also essential to give the executing thread with the TTL update the highest priority in the system to minimize the possibility of losing the lock due to host processor overload [6].

The above techniques allow to minimize errors when working with distributed blockers. However, it is clear that adding a distributed blocker to a project is not an easy task.

3.4 Application of Distributed Blockers to Worker Processes

Cron Worker

The simplest type of process worker in terms of taking a lock is a cron worker. This is due to the fact that the execution of the iteration of the cron worker is tied to the current time of the host, it is deterministic and does not depend on the start time of the application service. If the cluster consists of two or more nodes, then, provided that the time on the nodes is synchronized, each node will try to take the lock at the same moment. Yes, a condition is set here – time synchronization. Synchronization does not mean that the time on all hosts should go, for example, according to Moscow time (UTC + 3), but that the process receives the same time when requesting time in UTC. It is good practice to measure time in UTC for any application. In this case, the system time does not depend on the time zone of the hosts. In distributed systems, there are practices when the software of the cluster nodes does not require time synchronization on the hosts, the condition is that the time course itself is not disturbed, i.e. time passed at the same speed on all nodes. In this case, the systems synchronize their logical clocks, reducing everything to the wording "happened before" or "happened after" [5]. This method is not applicable to cron worker. However, worker processes do not impose requirements in the form of ensuring high accuracy of iterations. The limit of accuracy can be considered 10^{-3} s. It can be provided by NTP servers, which are currently used everywhere and are supported by every operating system [7]. Moreover, distributed blockers require time synchronization on hosts via NTP, and in the current work, distributed blockers are the main dependency. Thus, at time T, all iterations will try to acquire a lock on the iteration's resource. To simplify, the type of lock is mutex. For one process, the lock will be acquired, and it will start processing data in its iteration. At the same time, the remaining nodes wait until the lock is released. The working node, as it works, extends the TTL locks. Before releasing the lock, the worker node must record that the current iteration completed successfully. And what "current iteration" means should be clear to the rest of the cluster nodes, for example, it can be the date of the iteration trigger in UNIXTIME format. When the lock is released, or expires by TTL (in case of a node failure), the next node that took the lock checks whether the current iteration was successful, depending on this, it decides to execute or wait for the next iteration (Fig. 1).

Recurrent Worker
In the case of the recurrent worker, the situation is a bit more complicated. There is no deterministic runtime here. The essence of the recurrent worker is that the launch occurs once in a fixed time interval T. In the case of a single node, the intervals are measured from the time the service was started. The main problem is that services on distributed nodes do not start at the same time. And under these conditions, they need to be synchronized by intervals, otherwise the requirement "one iteration per fixed time interval" will be violated. This requirement applies to the entire cluster. Thus, the nodes need to agree on when the first iteration was. However, this is not necessary, the recurrent worker can be reduced to a cron worker, i.e. determine the exact date of the next iteration. Here it is necessary to mention that the cron worker has a minimum execution time interval equal to a second, which is due to the specifics of cron. A recurrent worker should not have such a limitation. In order to determine the date and time of the next iteration, service need to know the date and time of the first iteration. Or take this date as a fixed constant, for example, the beginning of time. Thus, the date and time of the next iteration can be calculated using the formula:

$$T_{next} = P\left[trunc\left(\frac{T_{current}}{P} \right) + 1 \right] \tag{1}$$

where T_{next} is the date and time of the next iteration, $T_{current}$ is the date and time now, P is the iteration period, *trunc* is a function that returns the integer part of the number.

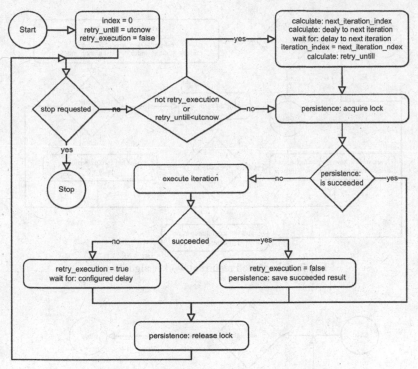

Fig. 1. A distributed cron worker algorithm.

Below is a C# (net6) function that calculates the date and time of the next iteration using the described formula. The described algorithm is illustrated in Fig. 2.

```
public DateTimeOffset CalculateNextExecutionDate(TimeSpan period, DateTimeOffset now)
{
    var numberOfFullPeriods = now.Ticks / period.Ticks + 1;
    return new DateTimeOffset(period.Ticks * numberOfFullPeriods, now.Offset);
}
```

Code. 1. A function that calculates the date and time of the next iteration.

Workload Worker

In the case of the workload worker, it will be necessary to use the key-value storage not only for locks, but also for its intended purpose. The fact is that the time of the next iteration depends directly on the execution time of the last iteration, the duration of the last interval between executions, value of the workload with which it ended, last delay and is iteration succeed. The next iteration time is calculated based on these five values by applying various formulas from the schedule settings. The details of the application of these formulas can be omitted. At the output they only have the date of the next iteration. In short, there, depending on the value of the workload, the length of time until the next iteration can increase, decrease, multiply, be set to a fixed value, etc.

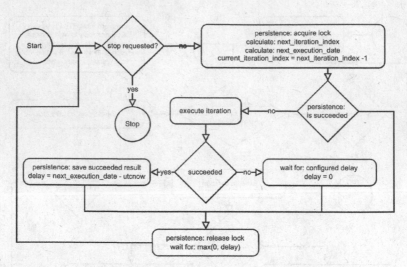

Fig. 2. Distributed recurrent worker algorithm.

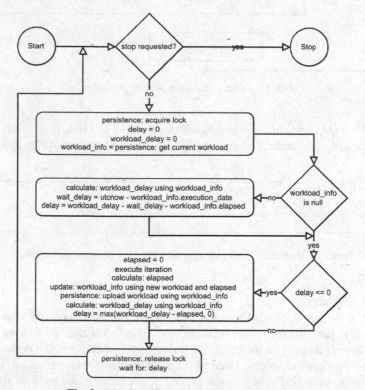

Fig. 3. Distributed workload worker algorithm.

In the Fig. 3 block diagram, the algorithm at the beginning of its work captures the lock by the process ID and receives the current information about the workload. Information data is received and updated only when the lock is active. Accordingly, if the current process ends with an error. Then the next process will receive up-to-date workload data and, based on this, calculate the launch date. If this is the first run and there is no information about the workload yet, then the algorithm starts iteration and captures the parameters and success of the iteration. After that, the iteration data is written to the storage, the lock is released, and the delay is calculated until the next iteration with the received parameters. Let's assume that the date of the next iteration is in a few hours. The current node knows about it. But as soon as the node releases the lock, it will immediately be taken over by another node. It will get information about the workload and calculate the delay until the next iteration. After that, it will release the lock and go into the waiting state until the next iteration. Because the calculation formulas are determined for all nodes, then the nodes will fight for the next block at the same time.

4 Discussion

Let's discuss the destabilizing factors and unexpected failures that the presented algorithms must cope with.

Most of the system's fault tolerance guarantees are provided by the key-value store itself. The presented algorithms are designed for peer-to-peer clusters that do not have a leader election mechanism. System nodes coordinate their actions through key-value storage. However, key-value stores that provide persistence, are generally not peer-to-peer. The key-value storage must have built-in protection against brain split (a situation where the storage nodes are separated by a network screen) [8].

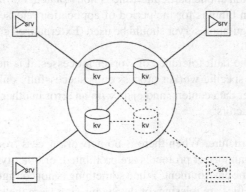

Fig. 4. General scheme of the whole system.

The diagram shows replicated key-value stores (Fig. 4). Each key-value store replica knows about the existence of other replicas. Replication is necessarily synchronous, because asynchronous replication will result in data loss upon failure and force service nodes to communicate only with the leader. Any service worker node can interact with any key-value store replica. Each node also knows about each node's key-value store. There are various discovery protocols for the service, sometimes they are specific to a particular key-value store, but usually this is either an explicit configuration or a DNS query. The service node can balance its requests between storage replicas, choosing the storage with the lowest ping. If one of the storage replicas is down, then the service will try to send a request to the next one.

In the case when a process has taken a lock and the server completely fails for some reason, then the next iteration in the system will start only when the TTL of this lock expires. Therefore, TTL must be set not too long, but not too short. For example, TTL is 1 s may not have time to update and then the node will lose its lock.

When a node fails, all three algorithms immediate starts the execution of the fallen iteration. For example, if it is a cron configured to iterate once a month, then this month the iteration must be performed. Therefore, in each type of worker (except workload) there is a concept about the iteration identifier and the success of its completion. If the time has come for the next iteration, and the current one was not completed successfully, then the whole system will already be performing a new iteration.

In the case of the situation mentioned above, when the TTL extension period was violated due to node overload, it is necessary to have a watchdog timer that will send a request to complete the iteration, since the lock is already owned by another process. Therefore, the TTL update period must be done once in TTL/k, where $k > 2$. Some blockers allow to create a "lease" for a certain value. And then, using the identifier of the received "lease", create keys and locks in the key-value store. And only one cycle is needed that will send a "heartbeat", extending the TTL of the lease. In the case when the lease is lost, then all distributed worker processes on the node stop working.

All of the above only work well if each node has an identical configuration file. It must be considered that if the nodes are configured differently, have different schedules, then the requirement for a certain iteration period will be violated. However, the requirement to perform one iteration at one particular time is not violated. For most data processing systems, violations in timings for the period of application release are acceptable. For other cases, the configuration server should be used (Externalized configuration pattern) [15].

When ensuring the fault tolerance of worker processes, it is necessary to consider the situation when a specific worker process ends successfully only in a certain set of nodes distributed over data centers, and ends with an error in other nodes. This may be due to a number of factors:

– Problem in infrastructure. When there is no network access from the data center to the resource, or a number of protocols are prohibited, or other types of firewalls.
– The problem is in the environment. When something is not configured in the operating system, necessary files are missing, or data is missing from the storages.
– Human factor. Configuration problem, system engineer error.

In this case, it is possible to increase the efficiency of the system as a whole by prioritizing cluster nodes according to business scenarios, specific worker processes, and node load. In solving this problem, the use of machine learning methods is proposed. Because In this paper, non-Byzantine distributed systems are considered (systems whose nodes do not distort information) [9, 9], then each node can keep a log of the success of operations, which will be processed by ML models to determine priority.

Ensuring process prioritization in a distributed blocker is not a trivial task that requires a separate study. Often, distributed blockers do not even support basic synchronization primitives, limiting themselves only to a mutex.

5 Conclusion

In this work, the definition of the worker process, their types and classification were given. The existing solutions for the implementation of worker processes are briefly considered. On examples close to reality, the problems of distributing worker processes across different servers are described. The features of using distributed blockers are described, as well as their application to all types of worker processes. A distributed worker configuration issue was mentioned. It also briefly describes ideas for organizing the prioritization of nodes by worker processes.

In further research, it is planned to carry out a series of activities, the purpose of which will be the developed library, using the methods described above. To achieve the goal, it is necessary to investigate the use of distributed blockers and evaluate their impact on system performance. Understand what types of blockers are suitable and appropriate for real fault tolerance.

References

1. Karunakar, R., Sahana, B., Akshay, N.P., Gautham, S., Dhanush, U.: Vertical scaling of virtual machines in cloud environment. In: 2021 International Conference on Recent Trends on Electronics, Information, Communication and Technology (2021)
2. Durgesh, R.: Deadlock in DBMS. Zenodo (2020)
3. Dawei, Y., Hengxiang, Y., Meihui, H., Jun, M.: Research on the application of distributed key-value storage technology in computer database platform. In: 2022 IEEE 2nd International Conference (2022)
4. Goetz Graefe, H., Jagàdish, V.: On Transactional Concurrency Control. Morgan & Claypool Publishers (2019)
5. Leslie Lamport: Specifying Systems (2003)
6. Brendan, B.: Designing Distributed Systems: Patterns and Paradigms for Scalable, Reliable Services (2018)
7. Tadayon, T.: Time Synchronization in Distributed Systems without a Central Clock (2019)
8. New, T., Yee, T.T., Htoon, E.C., Nakamura, J.: A consistent replica selection approach for distributed key-value storage system. In: 2019 International Conference on Advanced Information Technologies (ICAIT) Advanced Information Technologies (ICAIT) (2019)
9. Bolfing, A.: Distributed Systems. Oxford University Press (2020)
10. Dragoi, C., Widder, J., Zufferey, D.: Programming at the Edge of Synchrony. Université Paris Descartes, HAL (2020)
11. Quartz.NET: https://www.quartz-scheduler.net/documentation/quartz-3.x/quick-start.html. Accessed 20 Mar 2022
12. Hangfire: https://www.hangfire.io/. Accessed 20 Mar 2022
13. FluentScheduler: https://github.com/fluentscheduler/FluentScheduler. Accessed 20 Mar 2022
14. Wikipedia – Workflow pattern: https://en.wikipedia.org/wiki/Workflow_pattern. Accessed 20 Mar 2022
15. Pattern: Externalized configuration: https://microservices.io/patterns/externalized-configuration.html. Accessed 20 Mar 2022

Functioning of the Thermal Memory Cell

O. V. Volodina[(✉)] [ID], D. O. Varlamov [ID], and A. A. Skvortsov [ID]

Moscow Polytechnic University, 38 Bolshaya Semenovskaya Street, Moscow 107023,
Russian Federation
moosbeere_0@mail.ru

Abstract. The development of an algorithm for studying the functioning of a
thermal memory cell (TCC) was based on the selection of the minimum sufficient
time intervals between heating and the start of heating to maintain the temperature
corresponding to the temperature of the logical "1", as well as determining the
required heating frequency at which overheating will not occur or, on the contrary,
supercooling of the thermal cell structure. The article gives an idea about the device
of the TNP. A schematic and technical description of the installation for studying
the effect of thermal memory is given. The development of the algorithm was
carried out taking into account the electrophysical properties of the structure of
the thermal cell and the capabilities of the installation. The content of the article
consists of a description of the stages of the study with the intermediate results of
the functioning of the TNP. As a result of the work carried out, software was created
for the specialized installation "Thermal Memory Cell", based on the developed
algorithm.

Keywords: Thermal cell memory · Metallization film · Thermal conductivity ·
Current pulse · Dynamic memory

1 Introduction

Thermal memory cell is a functional element of thermal memory [1]. Such memory stores
data thermally, by maintaining the temperature. There are different types of memory:
dynamic and persistent. Persistent memory devices include CDs, hard drives, static
random access memory (SRAM). Dynamic memory is distinguished from permanent
memory by the presence of a process of regeneration of stored information. A well-
known dynamic memory device is DRAM chips of various types. They consist of a
matrix of cells assembled on a capacitor and a control transistor. A digital bit of data is
stored in the form of an electrical charge accumulated between the plates of a capacitor.
The charge eventually leaks from the plates and the capacitor is discharged. In order
not to lose the stored data, the capacitors must be constantly charged again. This is
the process of memory regeneration on capacitors. The study is aimed at creating a
conceptually new memory cell, a bit of information on which will be encoded in the
form of "heat". This form is also characterized by a dynamic change in the physical
state, namely heating and cooling.

A. Gibadullin (Ed.): ITIDMS 2021, CCIS 1703, pp. 42–56, 2022.
https://doi.org/10.1007/978-3-031-21340-3_5

2 Materials and Methods

2.1 Structure Description

A previously developed structure was used as a thermal cell - a metallization system - a thin metal film deposited on a semiconductor surface [2, 6, 8]. The schematic representation of the structure is shown in Fig. 1a, here the width of the metallization track is 75 μm, the length is $4*10^3$ μm. The thickness of the metallization film is 2…3 μm. The length of the semiconductor base of the structure is 104 μm, the width is $5*10^3$ μm. The track from contact I to I is designed to carry a current pulse in the forward and reverse directions. Contacts from 1 to 12 allow you to register a voltage signal from various sections of the conductive track. An electrophysical setup, hereinafter simply a setup, for studying the effect of thermal memory of the structure is shown in Fig. 1b. Here, the structure is fixedly fixed on a silicon substrate, to which current-carrying wires are soldered.

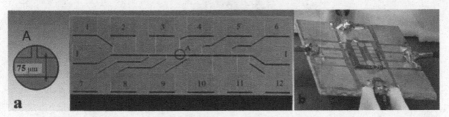

Fig. 1. Thermal memory cell internals: a) Schematic representation of the structure. b) Electrophysical installation.

2.2 Description of Impulse Installation

To study the effect of thermal memory of the electrophysical installation, a pulsed installation was designed and built using electronic components (see Fig. 2).

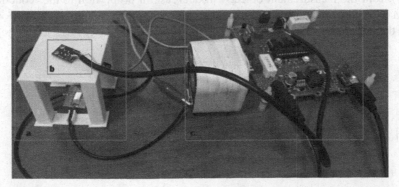

Fig. 2. Impulse installation: a) Thermal memory cell. b) IR thermometer. c) Control block.

The thermal memory cell (see Fig. 2a) consists of a holding structure in which an electrophysical installation is rigidly fixed with an infrared sensor located above it for temperature measurement.

IR thermometer. For the task in question, this pulsed installation uses an infrared thermometer for temperature measurement (pyrometer) Melexis MLX90614CI, (see Fig. 3). The objective angle of this pyrometer is 5o. Both IR-sensitive detector microcircuits, thermopile and ASSP signal conditioner are integrated into one TO-39 bank. Thanks to the low-noise amplifier, 17-bit ADC and powerful DSP block, high accuracy and resolution of the thermometer is achieved.

Fig. 3. IR thermometer Melexis MLX90614CI.

Estimated object and ambient temperatures are available in MLX90302 RAM with a resolution of 0.01 °C. They are available over a 2-wire SMBus serial bus with a compatible protocol (0.02 °C resolution). The measured value is the average temperature of all objects in the sensor's field of view. The MLX90614CI provides a standard accuracy of ± 0.5 °C at room temperature. The pyrometer is fixed for clarity at a distance of $3*10^2$ μm above the setup (see Fig. 2b). The optical system forms the field of view of the pyrometer, a region of space within which the temperature is measured (see Fig. 4). For correct measurements, it is necessary that the object completely covers the field of view. Otherwise, firstly, the thermal radiation flux falling on the pyrometer receiver (sensor) from the measurement object will decrease in proportion to the reduction in the area covered by the object, and secondly, the background radiation (objects located behind the measurement object) will fall on the receiver.

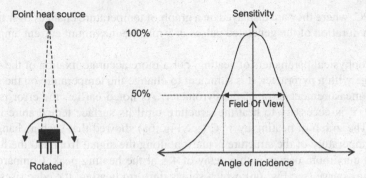

Fig. 4. Formation of the field of view of the IR thermometer.

A calculation was made of the distance between the object and the pyrometer necessary to obtain highly accurate measurements of the temperature of the plating track described above. According to the rule of a right-angled triangle, we find the value of the leg, which represents half the distance from the object to the pyrometer, the leg is indicated by the letter l in Fig. 5.

$$l = f \tan \beta = \frac{75}{2} \tan(90 - 2, 5) = 862, 5 \, \text{MKM} = 0, 86 \, \text{MM} \tag{1}$$

From here we get that the distance will be equal to:

$$L = l * 2 = 0, 86 * 2 = 1, 72 \, \text{MM} \tag{2}$$

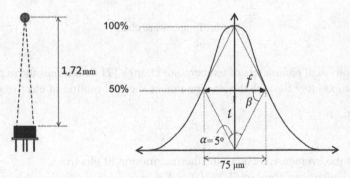

Fig. 5. Calculation of the distance between the object and an IR thermometer.

Calculations showed that in order to obtain the most accurate measurements of the temperature of an object, it is sufficient to place the pyrometer at a distance of 1.72 mm from the installation.

Control block. The control unit (see Fig. 2c) generates current pulses of different amplitudes and durations, controls the logic of sending pulses to the installation, and polls the pyrometer every second. The obtained measurements from the pyrometer are sent to a PC, where they are displayed on a graph of temperature changes over time. The maximum duration of the generated pulses is 5 ms, the maximum current amplitude is 20 A.

Electrophysical parameters of heating. For a more accurate fixation of the temperature change with a pyrometer, it is sufficient to change the temperature on the structure twice the measurement error of the pyrometer. As noted earlier, the error is 0.5 °C. Therefore, it is necessary to heat the structure until its surface temperature increases by 1 °C. The graph of heating by 1 °C (see Fig. 6a) showed that such a change in the surface temperature of the structure is uneven along the signal front and the formation of a point maximum occurs with a delay of 4 s at the heating peak. Compared to the 2 °C heating curve (see Fig. 6b), which shows uniform heating, the edge rises linearly to a point maximum.

We associate the unevenness of heating at the minimum possible temperature change with the difference in the measurement frequency and the change in the cooling rate. Those. the moments of receiving readings from the pyrometer appear corresponding to the rate of cooling at the temperature that will be obtained the next time the pyrometer is accessed.

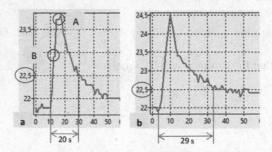

Fig. 6. Temperature chart.

Electrophysical parameters of temperature change [7] determines the expression of the body temperature through the average rate of thermal motion of electrons T:

$$T = \frac{u_T^2}{3k} \tag{3}$$

where u_T is the average velocity of the thermal motion of electrons;

k is the Boltzmann constant, $1.38*10^{-23}$ J/K^{-1};

m_0 is the electron mass, $0.91*10^{-30}$ kg.

As well as determining the rate of cooling at the border with air through the heat transfer coefficient m:

$$m = (\frac{\alpha * u}{\lambda * f})^{0.5} \tag{4}$$

mwhere α is the coefficient of heat transfer from the surface of the rod to the environment (air with a temperature of ~ 22 °C);

u is the surface perimeter;

λ is the thermal conductivity of aluminum (236 W/(m*deg) at room temperature);

f is the cross-sectional area of the aluminum film, taking into account the linear dependence of the heat transfer coefficient on the body temperature and ambient temperature.

At this stage of research, taking into account the results obtained, it was decided to heat the structure by 2 °C to reduce the effect of ambient temperature and limit the dependence on the pyrometer sampling rate.

The necessary heating on the used pulse installation could be achieved in several ways: by changing the amplitude of the current pulse, changing the duration of the pulse or the number of current pulses in a row with a frequency of 0.02 ms^{-1}. The use of an amplitude less than $2*10^{10}$ A/m^2 requires an increase in the number and duration of current pulses, which affects the heating period of the structure. Modern trends [3] to speed up memory cells require looking for the most optimal temporal characteristics of the operation of a thermal memory cell, such as heating time, access period for "reading", heating time, shown on the model of the time diagram of the TNP operation (see Fig. 7).

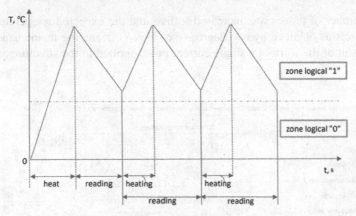

Fig. 7. Timing diagram of thermal memory cell operation.

Therefore, the current amplitude was increased to $2.5*10^{10}$ A/m^2 and the pulse duration was chosen to be 1 ms. An increase in electric power in the operation of semiconductor structures contributes to the development of degradation of metallization systems up to their melting [4]. Thermal memory is dynamic, i.e. it cannot permanently store the data written to it without periodically overwriting it. Such rewriting is possible only under conditions of constant maintenance of heat through heating. The heating process is implemented by passing current pulses through the structure with a certain frequency. What can be classified as "harsh" operating conditions, so the decision was made to no longer increase the amplitude of the current pulse. Further experiments were aimed at selecting the optimal number of heating and heating pulses.

Determination of the number of pulses. The application of three current pulses to the structure resulted in heating by one degree, which does not correspond to the conditions (see Fig. 8). Here, the maintenance of heat was the result of the work of two current pulses applied to the structure at a certain frequency. This graph corresponds to the simulated time diagram of the TNP operation (see Fig. 7).

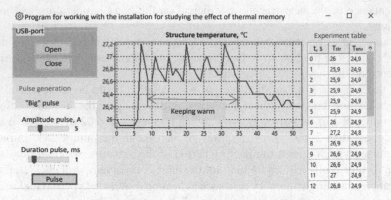

Fig. 8. Heating by 1° with 3 current pulses.

The number of pulses was increased to five and the expected temperature rise of the structure was obtained by two degrees (see Fig. 9). Here, the maintenance of heat was the result of the work of a single current pulse applied to the structure at a certain frequency.

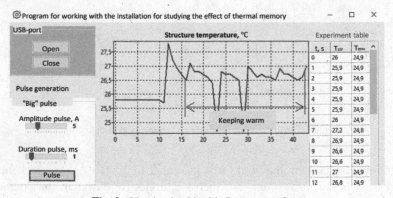

Fig. 9. Heating by 2° with 5 current pulses.

On the chart Fig. 9 shows sharp drops in temperature, which we associate with the measurement error of the pyrometer. To eliminate such interference in the operation of the TNC, it is necessary to maintain a temperature level at which the graph of temperature change from time to time will occupy 2/3 of the zone of the logical "1" (see Fig. 7).

Increasing the number of pulses to ten caused the structure to heat up by three degrees (see Fig. 10). The cooling rate during such heating is comparable to the cooling rate when heated by two degrees, but an increase in the heating time will lead to an increase in the "waiting" period for the thermal cell, when it cannot be accessed.

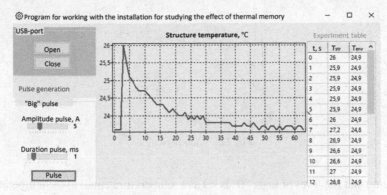

t, s	T_{str}	T_{env}
0	26	24,9
1	25,9	24,9
2	25,9	24,9
3	25,9	24,9
4	25,9	24,9
5	25,9	24,9
6	26	24,9
7	27,2	24,8
8	26,9	24,9
9	26,6	24,9
10	26,6	24,9
11	27	24,9
12	26,8	24,9

Fig. 10. Heating by 3° with 10 current pulses.

As a result of this stage of the study, the following physical parameters of the current were found: the amplitude of the heating and heating pulses - $2.5 * 10^{10}$ A / m^2, the duration of the heating and heating pulses - 1 ms, the number of heating pulses - 5 pcs, the number of heating pulses - 2 pcs initialization. The next stage of the study is aimed at determining the cell initialization period and the frequency of heating to maintain heat and save the recorded logical "1".

It is obvious that the higher the heating, the longer will be the cooling down to the initial temperature or the temperature close to the initial temperature by an order of magnitude of the pyrometer measurement error. But, as we found out, it is necessary to heat the structure by at least 2 °C to reduce the probability of a temperature drop below the logical "0" level. The considered graphs show that in order to speed up the operation of the thermal cell, it is necessary to set the level of logical "0" different from the initial temperature.

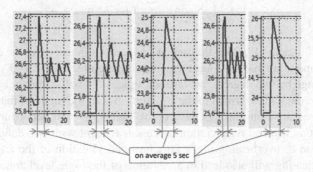

Fig. 11. Collection of temperature charts.

The graphs of temperature changes accumulated during the study period (see Fig. 11) show that rapid linear cooling occurs on average 5 s after the structure is heated. Therefore, it is possible to fix the temperature value of the structure 5 s after heating (T_{str5}) and from this value to calculate the temperature corresponding to the level of logical "0".

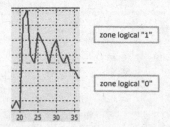

Fig. 12. Zone logical.

Assume that the level of logic "0" is set at a temperature equal to the temperature of the structure 5 s after heating. The graph (see Fig. 12) shows that in this case there is a possibility of a false transition to the logical "0" zone. Therefore, the level of logical "0" is taken to be the temperature value 0.3 °C less than the temperature Tstr5. Observation of the structure in the mode of keeping the logical "1" for 7.5 minutes (see Fig. 13) showed that there is no probability of a false positive. Here Tstr5 = 26.9 °C. The cooling rate to the level of logical "0" is 5 s.

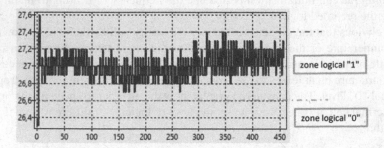

Fig. 13. Storing logic 1 for 7.5 min.

The level of logical "1", after discussions and long-term testing of the cell, is usually formed at a temperature that is 0.8 more than the temperature of logical "0". Since heating occurs on average by two degrees, the level of logical "1" will certainly be overcome at the moment the data bit is written to the structure. But in the mode of maintaining heat on the cell, false transitions through the level of logical "1" will not occur in this mode.

Regeneration. The cell regeneration process is fraught with two dangers. Frequent heating will lead to overheating of the structure and violation of the zones of logical levels. A rare heating will also lead to a violation of the logic level zones, but already due to a temperature drop on the structure. The graph of temperature versus time is shown in Fig. 14 obtained as a result of heating every 2 s. The research interval here is 60 s, which is enough to estimate the temperature increase.

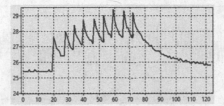

Fig. 14. Heating every 2 s.

Heating every 7 s (see Fig. 15) causes the structure to gradually cool down. Considering the cool-down time to logic zero of 5 s, we conducted a study with heating every 4 s for 5 min (see Fig. 16). The resulting graph satisfies the condition of location in the zone of logical "1". Since the less frequently the temperature is regenerated on the cell, the less is the risk of overheating the nanofilm, we conducted an experiment with heating every 5 s. The graph shown in Fig. 17a formed within 4 min. This graph also satisfied the condition of location in the zone of logical "1".

Fig. 15. Heating every 7 s.

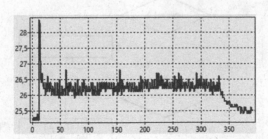

Fig. 16. Heating every 4 s for 5 min.

Continuing the test for 7 min confirmed that the set operating mode maintains the temperature change in the logical "1" zone (see Fig. 17b). This result satisfied all conditions and reduced the risk of overheating of the structure.

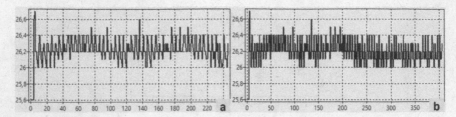

Fig. 17. Heating every 5 s.

3   Results

As a result of the study, the cell initialization period necessary for the formation of logical levels was found, it was 6 s. The initialization period is necessary to take into account the initial temperature of the structure, which depends on the ambient temperature. Reading information from a cell is possible immediately after initialization, i.e. after 6 s. The frequency of heat regeneration on the cell, the process of maintaining the temperature in the logical "1" zone, is 0.2 s-1. During the heating of the structure, the cell remains available for temperature reading (data acquisition).

On the basis of the obtained characteristics of the operation of the thermal cell, a block diagram of the algorithm for the functioning of the thermal cell was developed. The block diagram is divided logically into two stages: initialization (see Fig. 18) and regeneration (see Fig. 19). This algorithm is implemented in Pascal.

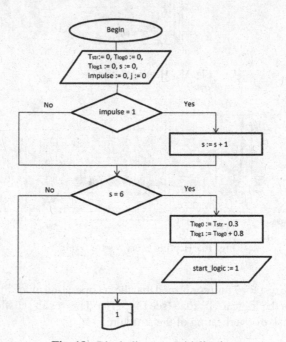

Fig. 18. Block diagram. Initialization.

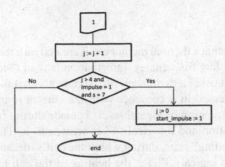

Fig. 19. Block diagram. Regeneration.

Processes are processed in the cycle of obtaining information from the pyrometer every second.

The result of the program operation is displayed on the PC screen (see Fig. 20) in the form of a graph of the temperature dependence of the structure over time and the corresponding timing diagram of switching logic levels. The interface also provides the ability to write a logical "0" or "1" to the thermal cell. Change the number of pulses or their amplitude. In the right window, you can view the values taken from the pyrometer: data reception time, structure temperature, ambient temperature, comments with information about the start of processes.

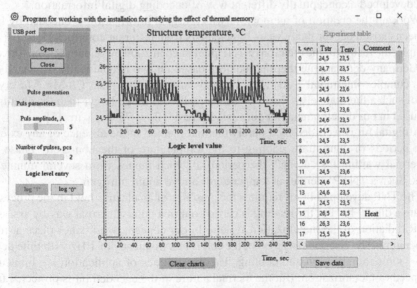

Fig. 20. Software interface.

4 Discussions

Our results have shown that a thermal memory cell created on a metallization system can successfully operate at low frequencies. Information is read thermally without loss of the stored bit on the cell using a pyrometer. Measurements are taken from the pyrometer every second and processed in accordance with the current temperature values of the logic levels. The determination of logical levels is made during initialization and when a cell is put into operation and a logical "1" is written to it. The initialization period puts the cell into a "pending" state, during which the cell's measured temperature is not processed. Recording a logical "1", i.e. the heating of the cell to a temperature of the logic level "1" is carried out by electric pulses passing through the metallization film in the amount of 5 pcs. After "writing" to the logical "0" cell, the "waiting" period is 5 s. This is the time for the temperature to drop to the value of logical "0" set during initialization. At this time, the processing of pyrometer measurements continues for a correct assessment of the speed of the TNP.

The developed software for a thermal memory cell in real time allows you to write and read bits of information. The correct operation of the cell can be monitored by the graph of the change in the temperature of the structure and the time diagram for switching logic levels.

This development shows that a bit of information can be physically represented in the form of "heat" along with electric charge in random access memory devices, "grooves" and "bases" on compact discs, a magnetic dipole on hard drives. Those. we have developed a conceptually different way of encoding digital information.

Work on the creation of memory, in which digital information is encoded by heat, has been carried out for many years by scientists from different countries [5, 9, 10]. For example, the results of the creation of TNP published in 2009 by scientists from Slovenia and Germany demonstrate thermal memory based on two magnetically frustrated systems: complex intermetal T-Al_3 (Mn, Fe) and canonical spin glass Cu-Mn. The crystal size of such a thermal cell is $2 \times 1 \times 1$ mm^3, which is much larger than the aluminum film used in our development, its dimensions are $4*10^3 \times 75 \times 3$ μm^3 [5].

A digital bit is recorded by a purely thermal method in the absence of any external field: periods of continuous cooling to the temperature of the non-erotic phase and isothermal waiting for "aging", the period of which ranges from several minutes to hours. Such a TNAP operates at temperatures above liquid nitrogen.

The TNP developed by us requires the presence of an electric field in the process of writing a digital bit, but the reading is carried out in a purely thermal way by assessing the IR radiation of the metallization system. In our concept, work takes place at room temperature. The "responsiveness" of the cell is at a frequency of 1 Hz with time delays of 5–6 s for initialization and cooling. The possibilities of application are limited by the speed of memorization. But the thermal nature of the encoded bit is protected from attack by cosmic rays and radiation. It is known that errors caused by cosmic rays pose a great danger to the dynamic and static memory modules installed in modern computers.

There is a limitation in the work of the TNP developed by us in terms of changing the ambient temperature after initialization. In the event of an increase in air temperature, the structure will heat up and the set logic levels will lose their relevance. Therefore, when working with TN, it is necessary to maintain the ambient temperature constant with an error of 1 °C.

5 Conclusion

In this study, we designed a thermal memory cell, considered the physical characteristics of its functioning, on the basis of which an algorithm was developed for programming a desktop interface for controlling a thermal memory cell. Before writing information to the TN, it goes through the initialization procedure for 6 s. Further, with a frequency of 0.2 Hz, heat is regenerated on the cell. After resetting the logical value on the cell to "0", it takes about 5 s until the logical "0" is fixed on the time diagram. For heating and maintaining heat, current pulses passing through the aluminum film with an amplitude of $2.5 * 10^{10}$ A / m^2 and a duration of 1 ms are responsible. The difference between the value of the level of logical "1" and the value of the level of logical "0" was 0.8 °C. The accepted physical parameters of the TN operation depend on its current implementation. And probably if you change the size of the metal film, then the speed of the heating and cooling processes will also change. But then, to select new parameters, it will be possible to use this article as a ready-made research algorithm for selecting key temperatures in the operation of the TNP, which will greatly simplify and speed up the process of creating another generation of TNP.

Our study, along with the studies of other scientists, clearly demonstrate the possibility of encoding a digital bit of information in the form of heat. Our development allows to encode 0 and 1 in thermal bits in real time and at ambient temperature.

In the future, we plan to create an analog-to-digital TN device that will not be tied to a PC. And on its basis to develop a dynamic thermal memory.

Funding. This work was supported by the Russian Science Foundation, project no. 22-29-01373.

References

1. Pshonkin, D.E., Volodina, O.V.: Temperature regimes of the "Heat cell" operation: in the collection "Collection of abstracts of the Ninth International Conference "Crystal Physics and deformation behavior of advanced materials", p. 154. published by NUST MISiS Moscow (2021)
2. Koryachko, M.V., Pshonkin, D.E., Skvortsov, A.A.: Features of Melt Droplet Formation during Electrical Destruction Aluminum Films on the Semiconductor Surface. Defect and Diffusion Forum, 410, pp. 737–741. Trans Tech Publications, Ltd. (2021)
3. Lin, C.-Y., et al.: A high-speed MIM resistive memory cell with an inherent vanadium selector. Applied Materials Today (2020)
4. Skvortsov, A.A., Kalenkov, S.G., Koryachko, M.V.: Article from the journal Phase transformations in metallization systems under non-stationary thermal action. Letters to ZhTF **40**(18), 24 (2014)
5. Dolinšek, J., Feuerbacher, M., Jagodič, M., Jagličić, Z., Heggen, M., Urban, K.: A thermal memory cell. Journal of Applied Physics **106**, 043917 (2009)
6. Pervikov, A., Toropkov, N., Kazantsev, S., Bakina, O., Glazkova, E.: Preparation of Nano/Micro Bimodal Aluminum Powder by Electrical Explosion of Wires. Lerner, Materials **14**(21), 6602 (2021)

7. Ripol-Saragosi, T.L., Kuusk, A.B.: Heat and mass transfer: a teaching aid for practical exercises, p. 28. State University of Communications (2019)
8. Mansurov, G.N., Petriy, O.A.: Electrochemistry of thin metal films, p. 51. MGOU, Moscow (2011)
9. Guarcello, C., Solinas, P., Braggio, A., Di Ventra, M., Giazott, F.: A Josephson thermal memory. Article in Physical Review Applie (2017)
10. Philippe, B.-A., Biehs, S.-A.: Near-Field Thermal Transistor, Phys. Rev. Lett. 112 (2014).

Using Data Mining Technology in Monitoring and Modeling the Epidemiological Situation of the Human Immunodeficiency Virus in Kazakhstan

A. D. Kubegenova⊕, E. S. Kubegenov⊕, Zh. M. Gumarova(✉)⊕,
Gaukhar A. Kamalova⊕, and G. M. Zhazykbaeva⊕

West Kazakhstan Agrarian Technical University named after Zhangir Khan, Uralsk 090009,
Kazakhstan

aina_zhg@mail.ru

Abstract. In this article, based on data mining technology, machine learning methods and cluster analysis, regularization of task identification is carried out, algorithms for numerically solving the inverse problem for a mathematical model for the spread of the socially significant disease human immunodeficiency virus in Kazakhstan are described. Data mining technology in modeling the situation with the human immunodeficiency virus is especially relevant, since it is on its basis that maps of the short-term incidence forecast in Kazakhstan and the regions of the country are compiled. The article discusses statistical data on the spread of the human immunodeficiency virus in Kazakhstan over the past 10 years (2010–2020). Information technologies, including Data mining technologies, allowed the authors to characterize the morbidity graph, identify risks, and test statistical predictors of morbidity. The main part of the article describes such indicators as an algorithm for numerically solving the inverse problem and building a mathematical model for the epidemiology of the human immunodeficiency virus by classifying regions into homogeneous groups. Data Mining classification methods were used to process the human immunodeficiency virus and analyze their status in the region. The forecast of the incidence of the population of Kazakhstan is carried out using the Statistica software package. An efficient algorithm for the numerical solution of the inverse problem for mathematical modeling will allow testing the developments on real data.

Keywords: Human immunodeficiency virus · Euclidean space · Cluster analysis · Data mining · Statistica advanced

1 Introduction

Currently, with the growth of HIV-infected people in Kazakhstan in public health, issues are increasingly emerging that require instant solutions and analysis of volumetric data. This problem entails, in addition to the danger of a pandemic nature, a wide range of social, medical and economic consequences that require prompt measures. The nature

A. Gibadullin (Ed.): ITIDMS 2021, CCIS 1703, pp. 57–65, 2022.
https://doi.org/10.1007/978-3-031-21340-3_6

of the danger of this disease lies in the defeat, first of all, of the young and able-bodied population of the republic.

According to UNAIDS experts (2021), there are more than 37.6 million people living with HIV in the world, of which 770 thousand have already died from AIDS-related diseases. Although the data of the joint UN program show the relative stability of the HIV pandemic, the incidence rate is still very high.

The coronavirus pandemic of 2019–2021 is a clear example of the danger of infections becoming uncontrolled, and showed all of humanity the tasks that can be overcome by the unprecedented measures of all states.

The problem of HIV infection, although it has a different distribution pattern, continues to be very dangerous, since the success of treatment has not yet led to the final recovery of patients in remission. According to the Republican Center for the Prevention and Control of AIDS, as of September 30, 2020, 27,100 cases of HIV infection were registered on an accrual basis, of which 16,344 were men, 10,756 were women, and 146 were children. In addition, 4,464 children born from women with a positive HIV status [1].

The new strategy of the Joint United Nations Program on HIV/AIDS (UNAIDS) has committed to ending the world's AIDS epidemic by 2030. This was reflected in the state program for the development of the healthcare system of the Republic of Kazakhstan "Health" for 2016–2030. The relevance of this issue is also caused by the need to study the nature of the HIV epidemic in Kazakhstan, especially in population groups with a high risk of infection.

In order to prevent the development of epidemiological outbreaks, methods of in-depth analysis are used that allow early detection of morbidity in the population. The medicine of Kazakhstan has come to understand the need to introduce statistical processing into all areas of its activity. However, with the widespread introduction of statistical processing tools, there came an understanding of the need not only for qualitative analysis, but also for a more detailed and in-depth study of data visualization processes. It is necessary not only to know the software package for statistical analysis, but also to specify them for each specific case. In this regard, conducting research related to medical data, with the study of the nature of morbidity in a whole group of people, should be determined by the integration of methods and a universal approach. The most important task of a researcher in conducting medical research is the choice of a specific method of statistical data analysis.

The scale and complexity of the health information system has increased dramatically, and its development and management is difficult to control. In the field of traditional methods and simple methods of mathematical statistics, it is difficult to solve the problems caused by the explosive growth of data and information, which will adversely affect the management of the medical information service system. Therefore, to guide the development and maintenance of software engineering, the collection of software data is especially important [1].

With the rapid development of computer and information technologies, as well as storage technologies, it becomes possible to store a large amount of data [2]. Data mining technology can search for and extract potentially valuable knowledge from large amounts of data. Database technology is the science of software that manages databases. The data from the database is analyzed by studying the methods of structuring, designing and applying the data [3]. With the rapid development of information technology, the scale, scope, and depth of database applications continue to expand, leading to the phenomenon of "rich data and bad information" [4]. Data mining is defined as the process of searching for a data pattern, that is, working with data from a large number of incomplete, fuzzy, random data. [5]. Data mining is a very active area of research in the field of databases and artificial intelligence [5–8]. strategies, contributing to sustainable development [9].

In data mining technology, the recognition parameters and the choice of coefficients are analyzed in detail, after which a data mining model is derived [10].

To analyze large anonymous data about patients, the authors propose to use a method based on the technology of processing and structuring case data. Using this method, it is possible to accurately and efficiently extract key information in each specific case using a special model [11]. An example of a mathematical model of epidemiology (co-infection with HIV and tuberculosis) shows studies on the identifiability of mathematical models [12]. The problem of identifying model parameters is reduced to minimizing the quadratic objective functional. Since nonlinear systems are considered, the solution of inverse problems of epidemiology can be ambiguous, therefore approaches to the analysis of the identifiability of inverse problems are described. These approaches make it possible to establish which of the unknown parameters (or their combinations) can be unambiguously and stably restored from the available additional information [13]. The coefficients of the epidemiological model describe the characteristics of the population and the development of the disease. The inverse problem of identifying parameters in a mathematical model is reduced to the problem of minimizing the objective function that characterizes the squared deviation of statistical data from experimental data. The set of statistical and optimization algorithms demonstrates the identification of parameters with the corresponding relative accuracy of 30%. The results can be used by healthcare organizations to predict the epidemic of infectious diseases in a given region by comparing simulation data with historical data [14].

The use of statistical methods for the analysis of medical information is currently not widespread in Kazakhstan, so the purpose of our research was to analyze, predict and predetermine the epidemiological situation using Data Mining technology.

2 Materials and Methods

As an object of study, data of a 10-year period (2010–2020) of the incidence of HIV infection in the Republic of Kazakhstan were selected. The classification of data on the incidence of the population was carried out using the analysis of Big Data Data Mining. As a tool for data analysis, we used the Statistica software package: StatisticaBase, StatisticaAdvanced, Data Mining data mining tools, and SANN automated neural networks. The latest clustering methods have made it possible to perform analysis using graphical forms, based on the single link method. Clustering of data by using graphical forms made it possible to reduce the time of analysis, as well as to develop an algorithm for predicting the incidence.

The practical significance and relevance of applying cluster analysis to data is beyond doubt, since in the modern information society, data and the results of their analysis play an increasingly important role, and clustering allows you to better understand these data.

3   Results and Discussion

The processing of experimental data was carried out on a computer in statistical packages.

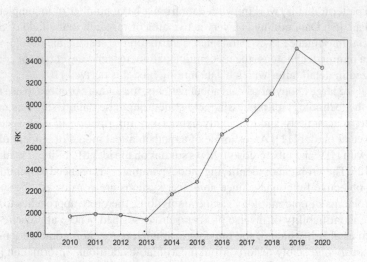

Fig. 1. Line chart of the Republic of Kazakhstan for 2010–2020.

A linear graph of the incidence (Fig. 1) of HIV infection (the number of patients and carriers) was built taking into account the aggregate data of a 10-year period for the population of the Republic of Kazakhstan (2010–2020). The abscissa axis shows the years of the study of HIV-infected people, the coordinate axis shows the absolute numbers of HIV-infected people (100,000 people). These diagrams show a steady trend in incidence over the period 2010–2013. Since 2014, the result has been deteriorating with a surge in incidence almost twice. In 2019, compared with the initial years of the study, the incidence of the population increases several times and reaches a kind of peak. However, by 2020 we are seeing a slight decrease in the incidence. This indicator is explained, on the one hand, by the deterioration of the information collection system during the pandemic of a new coronovirus infection, and, on the other hand, by its consequences in the form of deaths. Thus, when assessing the long-term dynamics of the incidence of HIV infection in the Republic of Kazakhstan, a rapid rise is revealed in the period from 2013 to 2019 and a decline in the time period 2019–2020.

The observed decrease in the vertical transmission path to 1.3% does not mean that this trend is absolute, since there is a fluctuation in it - the improvement in results is followed by a gradual deterioration. Based on the analysis of the linear graph according to the incidence rate of HIV-infected people, three groups of years can be distinguished:

– Years of moderate recovery (2010–2013);
– Years of high growth (2013–2019);
– Recession years (2019–2020) and 4) interim years (2014, 2016, 2018).

The sample mean value of the observed variable is determined by formula (1):

$$\bar{x} = \frac{i \sum_{i=1}^{n} x_i}{n} \tag{1}$$

where n is the sample size (true number of observations of variable x).

The median consists of two equal, ordered values divided evenly above and below. The mode is the most frequently occurring value in the dataset.

Sample variance characterizes the variability of a variable and is calculated by formula (2):

$$\bar{S}_x^2 = \frac{\sum_{i=1}^{n} (x_i - \bar{x})^2}{n-1} \tag{2}$$

where $\bar{x}$ is the sample mean.

The variance varies from 0 to infinity. The last value of 0 means no variability - the variables are constant.

The original data file contains information about HIV-infected people in 16 regions and 2 cities of the Republic of Kazakhstan. The purpose of this cluster analysis is to break into clusters and identify the corresponding cluster to identify risk groups. The use of cluster analysis to solve this problem is considered one of the main effective and widely used methods.

We will classify 16 regions using a hierarchical cluster analysis procedure, using the Euclidean distance (Euclideandistances) as a proximity measure, and the SingleLinkage method or the (near neighbors) method to unite clusters. With these methods, you can link two clusters together. When any two clusters are together, they get closer to each other and differ from the link distance. Accordingly, clusters linked together become separate elements, accidentally found together from the rest. This phenomenon strings objects together and forms clusters. The resulting clusters are represented by long chains. The determination of the natural number of clusters was carried out by combining regions into clusters. The order of combining regions into clusters is shown in a hierarchical tree (Fig. 2).

$$\pi = \frac{a_i + a_j}{2b_{iJ}} \tag{3}$$

where a_i, a_j are the average intracluster class distances; $i: j$; b_{ij} - average intercluster distances between the same classes. The estimate of the natural partition is made according to the following formula:

$$S = \frac{1}{k} \sum_{i=1}^{\bar{e}} \max \pi ij \tag{4}$$

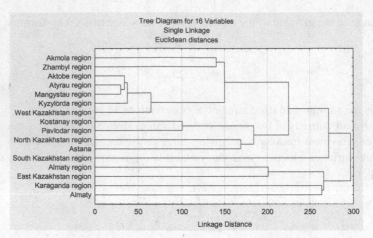

Fig. 2. Classification of the regions of the Republic of Kazakhstan by the incidence of the population from 2010 to 2020.

Identical values in objects are taken equal to one. The breakdowns obtained using the above algorithm will be equal to one or no more than 1. Accordingly, we can conclude that all objects, united into one cluster, ultimately equal one.

The SingleLinkade method is the most conceptual method, with the more common name of the Nearest-Neighbor method. The work of the algorithm is represented by the search for the two closest objects, the combination of which goes with the formation of the primary cluster. Each subsequent object joins the cluster to which this object is closer.

To determine the natural number of clusters into which collections of objects are divided, at each level of hierarchical clustering, the set was divided into a given number of classes. With each pair of clusters, the degree of their internal connection with each other was assessed. From here comes the calculation of the average intracluster distance for each cluster.

The ratio of the average intra-cluster distance to the inter-cluster distance is taken as an estimate of connectivity.

On the dendrogram, the distances (in arbitrary units) are marked along the horizontal lines, at which the objects are combined into clusters. The horizontal axis represents the observations, the vertical one - the distance of the association.

At the first steps, clusters of regions of Kazakhstan are formed: (Atyrauregion, Mangystauregion, Aktoberegion). Further clusters are formed (WestKazakhstanregion, Kyzylordaregion) - there are more clusters between these regions than between those that were merged in the previous steps. The following clusters - (Pavlodarregion, Kostanayregion) are combined into clusters (NorthKazakhstanregion, Astana). Further, clusters (Karagandaregion, Almaty) and (Akmolaregion, EastKazakhstanregion), etc. are combined into one cluster. The process ends with the union of all objects into one cluster. So, judging by the dendrogram, in this case, three clusters can be distinguished (Table 1).

Table 1. Matrix of Euclidean distances between clusters.

	Cluster 1	Cluster 2	Cluster 3
Cluster 1	0.0000	30,464.68	101,881.3
Cluster 2	174.5413	0.00	21,707.3
Cluster 3	319.1884	147.33	0.0

Table 2. Composition and content of clusters by incidence of the population of the Republic of Kazakhstan for a 10-year period (2010–2020).

Cluster No	Cluster filling, units	Cluster Composition
1	4	Almaty region, Karaganda region, East Kazakhstan region, Almaty region
2	5	South Kazakhstan region, Astana city, North Kazakhstan region, Pavlodar region, Kustanai region
3	7	West Kazakhstan region, Kyzylorda region, Mangistau region, Atyrau region, Aktobe region, Zhambyl region, Akmola region

Figure 3 illustrates that when the proximity measure is cut off at the level of 250, 3 clusters stand out. The composition of the resulting clusters is determined in Table 2.

After analyzing the features of the obtained clusters and comparing the average values of HIV-infected persons by class in the regions, we obtained the following results:

The first cluster as a whole is characterized by an average level of HIV infection among the adult population and vulnerable groups of the population - drug users, convicts, and occupies the share of sexual transmission of HIV infection;

The second cluster is characterized by a low rate of HIV infection compared to cluster 1. The second cluster includes a group of people who are at high risk, however, suffering from alcoholism, drug addiction and other social diseases;

The third cluster shows the incidence and route of transmission of HIV infection among injecting drug users, as well as those infected through sexual transmission and intrauterine transmission from a sick mother to the fetus. Figure 4 also shows significant differences in relation to the three groups of regions.

Results of tree clustering. Steps are plotted along the horizontal axis on the diagram, distances are plotted along the vertical axis. In total, the algorithm took 16 steps to combine all objects into one cluster.

The resulting classification revealed clusters with a high growth of HIV-infected people in the regions united in cluster 1. The results of statistical forecasting obtained by combining regions into homogeneous groups and solving inverse problems showed that injecting drug users are predictors of incidence. Processing with the help of Data mining

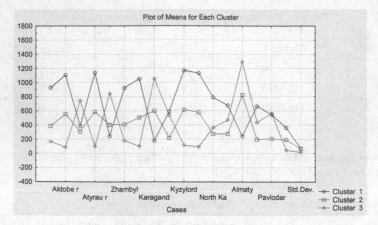

Fig. 3. Graph of average values for each cluster.

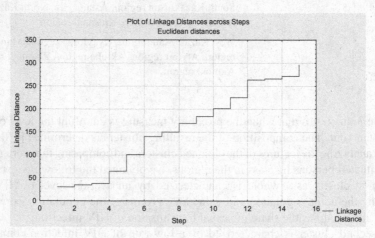

Fig. 4. Graph of the association scheme by steps.

showed that this population group continues to stimulate the growth of the HIV epidemic. The increase in the proportion of coinfections, in the structure of which sexually transmitted infections play an important role, causes serious concern .

4 Conclusion

Thus, the following conclusions can be drawn from the results of the study:

- The analysis of the incidence of HIV in the Republic of Kazakhstan over a 10-year period (2010-2020) revealed a sharp increase in HIV-infected people and a steady trend in incidence.
- The cluster classification algorithm revealed the internal connectivity between objects and showed the correctness of the mathematical model of HIV epidemiology.

- Processing with the help of Datamining showed a continuing increase in the incidence of HIV infection in Kazakhstan.
- The results of statistical forecasting revealed the predictors of morbidity, causing a high risk group and stimulating the growth of the HIV epidemic.
- Clustering and the nature of the resulting clusters will make it possible to form from their aggregates a special base for modeling, optimizing and selecting specific antiretroviral drugs and therapeutic regimens in the fight against HIV infection in Kazakhstan.

References

1. Statistical collection: Health of the population of the Republic of Kazakhstan and the activities of healthcare organizations in 2020. https://amanbol.kz/news/vich-v-kazakhstane-dannye/https://masa.media/ru/site/
2. Cui, Z., Yan, C.: Deep Integration of health information service system and data mining analysis technology. Applied Mathematics and Nonlinear Sciences **5**(2), 443–452 (2020)
3. Xinyi, W.: The role of data mining technology in advertising marketing. J. Phys.: Conf. Ser. **1744**, 042202 (2021)
4. Yang, J., Li, Y., Liu, Q.: Brief introduction of medical database and data mining technology in big data era. J Evid Based Med. **13**, 57–69 (2021)
5. Jianguo, L., Sheng, Z.: Application research of data mining technology in personal privacy protection and material data analysis. Integrated Ferroelectrics **216**(1), 29–42 (2021)
6. Bijalwan, V., Kumar, V., Kumari, P.: KNN based machine learning approach for text and document mining. Int. J. Database Theory and Application **7**(1), 61–70 (2014)
7. Yukselturk, E., Ozekes, S., Turel, Y.K.: Predicting dropout student: an application of data mining methods in an online education program. European Journal of Open, Distance and e-learning **17**(1), 118–133 (2014)
8. He, W., Yan, G., Xu, L.D.: Developing vehicular data cloud services in the IoT environment. IEEE transactionsonindustrialinformatics **10**(2), pp. 1587–1595 (2014)
9. Peña-Ayala, A.: Educational data mining: A survey and a data mining-based analysis of recent works. Expertsystemswith applications **41**(4), 1432–1462 (2014)
10. Liu, L.: Development and Application of Computer Data Mining Technology. In: International Conference on Applications and Techniques in Cyber Intelligence ATCI 2019. ATCI 2019. Advances in Intelligent Systems and Computing, 1017. Springer, Cham (2020)
11. Liu, M., Qu, M., Zhao, B.: Research and citation analysis of data mining technology based on bayes algorithm. Mobile Netw Appl **22**, 418–426 (2017). https://doi.org/10.1007/s11036-016-0797-2
12. Zhenhua, H., et al.: Analysis of COVID-19 spread characteristics and infection numbers based on large-scale structured case data. Scientia Sinica Informationis **50**(12), 1882 (2020)
13. Kabanikhin, S.I.: Determination of the coefficients of nonlinear ordinary differential equations systems using additional statistical information. Int. J. Mathe. Physics **10**(1), 36–42 (2019)
14. Kabanikhin, S.I., Krivorotko, O.I.: Mathematical Modeling of the Wuhan COVID-2019 Epidemic and Inverse Problems. Comput. Math. and Math. Phys. **60**, 1889–1899 (2020). https://doi.org/10.1134/S0965542520110068
15. Kabanikhin, S., Olga, K., Victoriya, K.: A combined numerical algorithm for reconstructing the mathematical model for tuberculosis transmission with control programs. Journal of Inverse and Ill-posed Problems **26**(1), 121-131 (2018)

Information Technology and Artificial Intelligence in Improving of Center Pivot Irrigation Control

G. Kamyshova[1]([⊠]) [iD], S. Ignar[2] [iD], and N. Terekhova[3] [iD]

[1] Financial University under the Government of the Russian Federation, Leningradskiy pr-d 49/2, 125167 Moscow, Russia
gnkamyshova@fa.ru

[2] Warsaw University of Life Sciences, Nowoursynowska street 159, 02-776 Warsaw, Poland

[3] Saratov State Agrarian University, Theatralnaia pl.1, 410012 Saratov, Russia

Abstract. The present study is focused on developing a center pivot irrigation control model that combines information technology and neuro-prediction. Modern digital technologies allow data collection, their analysis and operational management of equipment and technological processes in real time, which allows, on the one hand, to apply new approaches to modeling technical systems and processes -the so-called "data-driven models". On the other hand, it requires the development of fundamentally new models, which will be based on artificial intelligence methods. Information technology allows real-time analysis of the tracks and actual speeds of the sprinkler, which shows their significant deviations. We have developed a sprinkler control model based on information technology, the theory of artificial neural networks and predictive control. The application of the model makes it possible to implement control algorithms with a prediction of the reaction of the sprinkler to the control signal. We propose a diagram of an algorithm for constructing a predictive control, the structure of a neuro-regulator and tools for its synthesis using modern software. It is possible to use the proposed model both to improve the efficiency of the management of existing equipment, and in the development of new sprinklers with integrated intelligent control systems.

Keywords: Artificial neural networks · Predictive control · Neuro-controller · Center pivot irrigation

1 Introduction

The growth of sown areas over the past half century has amounted to about 12%, which has led to an almost threefold increase in agricultural production. An increase in production can take place on the available cultivated lands largely due to its intensification. At the same time, the role of irrigation increases, since irrigated lands account for more than 40% of the growth in world food production and 60% of grain production. Climate change, shrinking agricultural land and lack of water resources are key challenges against the backdrop of rapidly increasing food demand. The agricultural sector is undergoing

A. Gibadullin (Ed.): ITIDMS 2021, CCIS 1703, pp. 66–78, 2022.
https://doi.org/10.1007/978-3-031-21340-3_7

a transformation driven by new technologies that will allow the sector to move to a new level of productivity. Precision agriculture, which consists in applying the necessary resources when and where needed, has become the third wave of the modern agricultural revolution. Currently, the use of digital and intelligent technologies is expanding due to the increase in the availability of large amounts of data and technologies for their processing. Big data is now being used to give farmers real-time predictive information about agricultural operations and operational decisions. Real-time artificial intelligence allows computer programs to generate detailed recommendations and insights to help farmers make the right decisions. Even though in Russia there is a significant potential of land and water resources for irrigated agriculture, it is possible to achieve a radical increase in the efficiency of agriculture in general and irrigated agriculture in particular only through digitalization and intellectualization. This is proved by the experience of the world's leading agrarian countries, for which the share of farms using digital technologies ranges from 60% (USA) to 80% (EU countries). And in Russia, according to experts, this is only 10%. At the same time, the overall level of digitalization is in fifteenth place in the world, and the level of digitalization of agriculture is in forty-fifth [1]. According to the International Institute for Food Policy Research, digital technologies can help us achieve a 67% increase in farm productivity by 2050 [2].

The technical support of irrigated agriculture is one of the central parameters of its effectiveness. In the last decade, in the most active way, multi-support circular sprinklers of foreign and domestic production are being introduced into irrigated agriculture. The development of digital technologies also has an impact on the development trends of sprinkler technology. One of the key areas is intellectualization, automation, and robotics. Among such techniques are examples of Zimmatic, Valley, Reinke, which are already actively following this path. This sprinkling technique has higher characteristics of irrigation automation and reliability, but at the same time it is also costly and often difficult to operate. An analysis of scientific research in the field of improving sprinkler technology in Russia shows their focus, first, on improving the design parameters [3, 4]. And only in the last few years, efforts have been made to introduce elements of automation and robotization into irrigation equipment [5].

Modern advances that contribute to the growth of data collection and analysis capabilities can significantly improve the efficiency of engineering solutions. To control technical objects, systems based on artificial intelligence methods such as artificial neural networks, machine learning algorithms and much more are increasingly used. Neural networks and control systems created on their basis (the so-called neurocontrol) are actively used in various fields of technology, such as, for example, motion control systems for robots, aircraft, ships, etc. [6, 7]. In recent years, a large amount of foreign research has focused on the application of data mining and deep learning methods to improve irrigation efficiency. Thus, E. Guisti and S. Marsili-Libele [8] developed an intelligent irrigation control system based on fuzzy logic, J. Navarro-Hel, J. Martinez del Ricon, R. Domingo-Minguel and F. Soto [9] decision support for irrigation management, H. Song, J. Jang, F. Li, Y. Zhao and J. Yang [10] investigated the spatiotemporal distribution of soil moisture. At the same time, intellectual and information technologies and irrigation technical means based on them still require further development. The works [11, 12] present approaches to the improvement of irrigation technology based on neurocontrol methods. However, it is necessary to intensify research in this area towards the creation of various models that combine modern information technologies and artificial intelligence to improve the efficiency of watering machines. The present study focuses on the development of a center pivot irrigation (CPI) control model that combines information technology and neuro-prediction.

2   Materials and Methods

The development of a model for the neuro-predictive control of center pivot irrigation (CPI) is based on the use of modern methods of artificial neural networks, neural network control models, information technology and technical means for collecting and analyzing data, as well as on the use of modern software products and programming languages such as Matlab, Python, etc. To collect data, experimental studies were carried out in the Engels district of the Saratov region on the basis of the UNPO of the Volga region of the Saratov State Agrarian University.

The irrigated area is equipped with the Cascade CPI system. It is equipped with GPS trackers, cameras and real-time data is displayed in the digital platform for managing agribusiness "Agrosignal". In addition, the Agrosignal system allows collecting data on the weather, soil conditions and basic agrotechnical information about crops, equipment operation based on weather station sensors, remote sensing, etc. (Fig. 1):

Weather - wind speed and direction, air temperature, relative humidity, temperature and humidity of foliage and soil, atmospheric pressure, amount of precipitation.

Indices - Normalized Relative Vegetation Index (NDVI), Normalized Difference Water Index (NDWI), Moisture Stress Index (MSI), Green Leaf Index (GLI).

CPI system status - speed.

Each CPI as part of the irrigation complex is located in a specific area with certain geo-coordinates, which leads to the presence of spatial variability of soil, geomorphological, hydrogeological conditions (Fig. 2). In addition, there may be spatio-temporal variability of both the agricultural crop and its phase of growth and development.

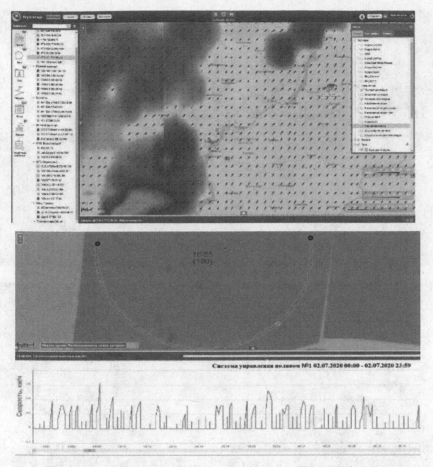

Fig. 1. Agrosignal system window - weather (top), CPI speed (bottom)

The key characteristic in irrigation is the irrigation rate. On the one hand, based on the hydraulic model of the sprinkler, the irrigation rate depends on the speed. On the other hand, this dependence remains and is significant during the operation of sprinkling machines ([13]), moreover, it is not linear and is due to many stochastic operational factors such as agricultural background, field slope, soil type, soil moisture, and much more.

Analysis of movement tracks and actual speeds of movement of the sprinkler in real time, both during the passage of a full circle of irrigation, and analysis of specific sectors throughout the entire season of work showed their significant deviations in the range of 8–13% of the set movement speed, which leads to deviations in irrigation rates by 7.4–11% from the specified ones.

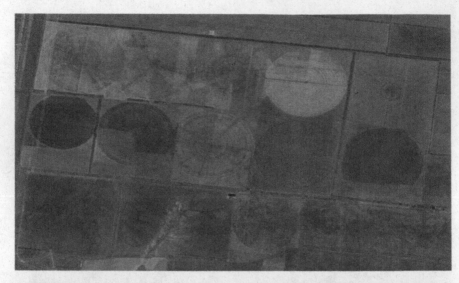

Fig. 2. Irrigation complex with CPI at the study site: image (top), CPI in the Agrosignal system (bottom)

Because the sprinkling machine is a complex dynamic object, and the irrigation process is a complex dynamic process with nonlinear relationships, we will use the so-called "data-driven approach" instead of the classical methods of mathematical modeling using an analytical description using differential equations of the object's behavior (models based on data). This approach allows using artificial intelligence methods, namely neural network methods and models. Modeling, which is based on artificial neural networks, considers the behavior of an object as a "black box", which has known inputs and outputs, and the task of the network is to "best imitate" its behavior.

A set of neurons connected by inputs and outputs make up a neural network, which has a mathematical formalization. The adder equation and the activation block equation are a formalization of an artificial neuron [14]:

$$s_k = \sum\nolimits_{j=1}^{n} w_{j,k} \cdot x_j + b_k \qquad (1)$$

and activation block equation

$$y_k = \phi(s_k), \qquad (2)$$

where, for k-th neuron, $x_1, x_2, ..., x_n$ - input signals; $w_{1,k}, w_{2,k}, ..., w_{n,k}$ - synoptic weights; b_k - reference signal level; s_k - linear adder output; $\phi(s_k)$ - activation block conversion function; y_k - output signal.

When developing a control system, it is possible to use artificial neural networks. The choice of specific methods and models from a huge number of neural network models and structures essentially depends on the problem being solved. However, the common thing in designing a model is the presence of the following steps:

1. Identification of a controlled process - development of a neuromodel of a controlled process.
2. Synthesis of the control law - the construction of a regulator based on a neuromodel.

For identification, a two-layer artificial neural network with delay lines is used. Information about the behavior of the sprinkler is used to train the model and adjust the weights of the artificial neural network based on one of the algorithms (for example, [15]). More significant is the second stage, on which our study is concentrated.

3   Results and Discussions

A detailed analysis of the actual speeds of the sprinkler (Fig. 3) in relation to geolocation throughout the entire season of work shows the presence of a certain relationship.

However, this dependence cannot be expressed by a simple analytical expression of the form $V(t) = F(X(t), Y(t), Z(t), ...)$, where X, Y, Z, etc. are some factors that affect the speed V. Either we must simplify the model and discard some of the parameters or linearize the dependencies. All of the above will result in a significant loss of accuracy. In addition, the model will be local in nature and its generalization will require significant resources.

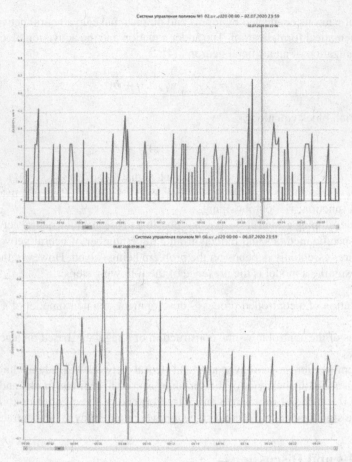

Fig. 3. Graphs of the actual speeds of movement of the CPI by dates of irrigation

Thus, the problem is to build a predictive model of the performance of the CPI (in our case, speed) and manage irrigation based on this model.

The model is a combination of two components: the first component is information technologies for collecting and analyzing data on the state of the control object and the operating environment (Agrosignal system). The second component of our system is based on intelligent technologies, which are based on neural network models of the speed of the sprinkler during irrigation and predictive control models of the CPI built on their basis. The conceptual diagram of the model is shown in Fig. 4.

The dynamics of the behavior of the CPI as a control object can be represented in a discrete form:

$$\begin{cases} X(k+1) = F(X(k), U(k)) \\ \quad V(k+1) = G(X(k), \end{cases}$$
(3)

where $X(k)$ is the value of the state vector and $U(k)$ is the value of the input (control) vector at the kth step, $V(k+1)$ is the value of the output vector (velocity) at the $(k+1)$th step.

The conceptual model of predictive control consists in determining the sequence of control actions (that is, controlled changes in input data) so that the predicted response moves to a given point in an optimal way [14]. All calculations are based on current measurements and projections of future sprinkler speed outputs. At a certain time interval in the future, the neural network speed control model predicts the response of the sprinkler. Let the actual output v, the predicted output $\hat{v}$ and the control action u. At the current time point, denoted by k, the model computes a set of M input data values $\{u(k+i-1), i = 1, 2, \ldots M\}$. The set consists of the current input control $u(k)$ and M $-$ 1 future inputs. The input remains constant after M-fold movement of the knob. The inputs are calculated so that the set P of predicted speed outputs $\{\hat{v}(k+i), i = 1, 2, \ldots P\}$ optimally reaches the given value. The control signal is calculated by the optimization block using the predicted outputs based on the optimization condition for the control quality functional [16]:

$$J = \sum_{i=n}^{l} \left(v_r(k+i) - v_f(k+i) \right)^2 +$$
(4)

$$\rho \sum_{i=1}^{q} (u(k+i-1) - u(k+i-2))^2 \xrightarrow{u} min$$
(5)

Here, the parameters n, l, q, ρ are model parameters that determine the limits for calculating the tracking error and the power of the control signal. The variable u describes the trial control signal on which the optimization takes place, v_r and v_f are the desired and actual speeds in the model. The control power is given by ρ. The number of predictions P is called the prediction horizon, and the number of controls moves M is called the control horizon. It is proposed to choose the prediction horizon in accordance with the number of sectors into whichhe total irrigation area is divided. Moreover, the larger the partition, the more accurate the overall forecast will be.

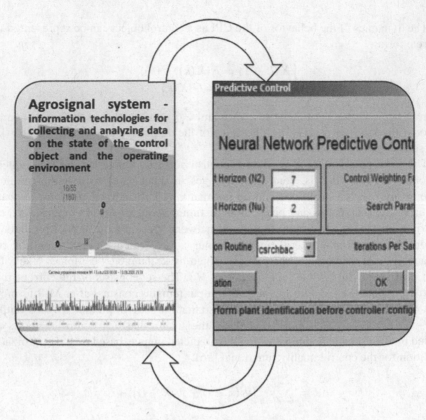

Fig. 4. Concept model diagram

The following algorithm for constructing a predictive control of a CPI is proposed (Fig. 5).

To introduce predictive neurocontrol into the general control system of the center pivot irrigation, based on the developed model and algorithm, a neuroregulator is created, which consists of an optimization block that calculates the optimal control values u^* according to the quality criterion J, and the signal corresponding to the value u^* controls the process.

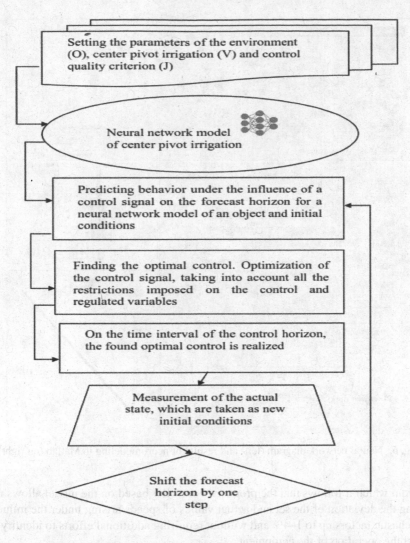

Fig. 5. Algorithm for constructing a predictive control of a CPI

The synthesis of the controller can be implemented, for example, in the Neural Network Blockset/Control Systems application package of the Matlab system using the NN Predictive Controller block [15]. In [17], the construction of such a general neuro-controller for the speed of a sprinkling machine was considered.

Simulation of the model of neuro-predictive CPI speed control shows its good convergence (Fig. 6).

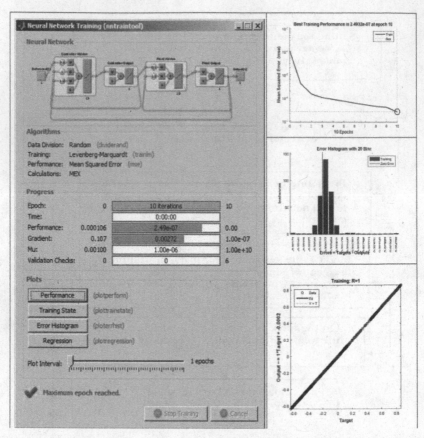

Fig. 6. Neural network diagram (left) and results of neuromodeling in Matlab (on right)

From which it follows that the proposed controller based on the model allows minimizing the deviation of the set and actual values of speeds arising under the influence of stochastic factors up to 1–4% and without requiring additional efforts to identify and correct the operation of the equipment.

4 Conclusions

A CPI control model based on a combination of information technology, predictive control approaches and the theory of artificial neural networks has been developed. The application of the model makes it possible to implement control algorithms with a prediction of the reaction of the sprinkler to the control signal. A scheme of an algorithm for constructing a predictive control, the structure of a neuro-regulator and tools for its synthesis are proposed.

The model based on neuro-predictive control allows to reduce the gap between the set and actual rate to 1–4%, as opposed to the existing 7–11%, which leads to an improvement in the efficiency and quality of irrigation. The model has versatility, which allows it to be used for different types of sprinklers and in different conditions. The model can be used to improve the efficiency of managing both existing equipment (introduction into decision support systems) and in the development of new sprinklers (direct integration into intelligent control systems of sprinklers and robotic irrigation systems).

References

1. Bogomolov, A., Nevezhin, V., Larionova, M., Piskun, E.: Review of digital technologies in agriculture as a factor that removes the growth limits to human civilization. E3S Web of Conferences **247**, 01074 (2021)
2. Trendov, N.M, Varas, S., Zeng, M.: Digital technologies in agriculture and rural areas. Food and Agriculture Organization of the United Nations. Rome (2019). https://www.fao.org/3/ca4887en/ca4887en.pdf. Access date: 5 April 2022
3. Olgarenko, G.V., Turapin, S.S.: Analytical studies of the prospects for the development of irrigation technology in Russia: Information and analytical publication. IP Lavrenov A.V., Kolomna (2020). (in Russian)
4. Olgarenko, G.V., Ugryumova, A.A., Kapustina, T.A., Zamahovsky, M.P.: Problems and prospects of food security in the regions of the Russian Federation. IOP Conf. Series: Earth and Environmental Science **317**, 012012 (2019)
5. Soloviev, D., Zhuravleva, L., Bakirov, S.: Robotic Irrigative Complex with Intellectual Control System "CASCADE". XVIII International Scientific and Practical Conference "Modern Trends in Agricultural Production in the World Economy" (2019)
6. Thomas, A., Hedley, J.: FumeBot: a deep convolutional neural network controlled robot. Robotics **8**, 62 (2019)
7. Cheon, K., Kim, J., Hamadache, M., Lee, D.: On replacing PID controller with deep learning controller for DC motor system. Journal of Automation Control Engineering. **3**(6), 452–456 (2015)
8. Giusti, E., Marsili –Libelli, S.: A Fuzzy decision support system for irrigation and water conservation in agriculture. Environmental Modeling & Software **63**, 73–86 (2014)
9. Navarro-Hellin, H., Martinez-del-Ricon, J., Domingo-Miguel, R., Soto-Valles, F., Torres-Sances, R.: A decision support system for managing irrigation in agriculture. Computers and Electronics in Agriculture **124**, 121–131 (2016)
10. Song, X., Zhang, G., Liu, F., Li, D., Zhao, Y., Yang, J.: Modeling spatio-temporal distribution of soil moisture by deep learning-based cellular automata model. Journal of Arid Land **8**, 734–748 (2016)
11. Soloviev, D.A., Kamyshova, G.N., Terekhova, N.N., Zatinatsky, S.V., Kolganov, D.A.: Improving the efficiency of circular irrigation machines based on models of neural network irrigation control. E3S Web of Conferences/INTERAGROMASH 2020, 175 (2020)
12. Kamyshova, G.N., Soloviov, D.A., Kolganov, D.A., Korsak, V.V., Terekhova, N.N.: Neuromodeling in irrigation management for sustainable agriculture. Advances in Dynamical Systems and Applications **16**(1), 159–170 (2021)
13. Soloviev, D.A., Zhuravleva, L.A.: Influence of the mode of movement of sprinkling machines on the rate of irrigation. Bulletin of the APK of the Upper Volga **1**(41), 38–43 (2018). (in Russian)

14. Haykin, S.: Handbook of Neural networks, 2 edition, p. 1104 (2016)
15. Beale, M., Hagan, M., Demuth, H.: Neural Network Toolbox User's Guide. The MathWorks. Natick (2015)
16. Domański, P.D.: Performance Assessment of Predictive Control—A Survey. Algorithms **13**(97), (2020)
17. Soloviev, D.A., Kamyshova, G.N., Terekhova, N.N., Bakirov, S.M.: Modeling of neurocontrol of the speed of sprinkling machines. Agrarian scientific journal **7**, 81–84 (2020)

KOA Pathology Screening Using Multi-channel VAG Signal Fusion Method

Chunyi Ma ⓘ and Jianhua Yang(✉) ⓘ

School of Automation, Northwestern Polytechnical University, Xi'an 710129, Shaanxi, China
yangjianhua@nwpu.edu.cn

Abstract. Knee Osteoarthritis (KOA) is a chronic degenerative lesion of the knee joint, which is difficult to detect clinically. However, the use of knee-joint vibroarthrographic (VAG) signal to assist clinical testing is an effective non-invasive method for KOA pathology diagnosis. In order to improve the correct rate of pathological diagnosis with VAG signals, this paper proposes a KOA pathological screening method using the multi-channel signal fusion method. This method can realize the VAG signal fusion with both high channel consistency and reliability, increase the difference of normal and abnormal VAG signal characteristics realized on the data, improve the KOA pathology screening accuracy by combining time-domain feature extraction and random forest classification methods to obtain features with more discrimination to categories when extracting features. The experimental results showed that this method could obtain high correct rates of KOA pathology screening, with accuracy, precision, and specificity of 0.95, 0.95, and 0.96, respectively, which can be used as an effective method for non-invasive computer-aided KOA diagnosis.

Keywords: Knee Osteoarthritis (KOA) · Vibroarthrographic signal · Multi-channel signal fusion · Pathological screening · Feature extraction · Random forest

1 Introduction

Knee joint injury is a common human injury and joint lesion [1]. As is well known, arthritic degeneration from injury to the knee joint is caused by various traumas. However, the non-traumatic patella can also lead to osteoarthritis, where the articular cartilage becomes soft, fibrotic and detaches from the patellar, femoral or tibial surfaces, leading to painful inflammation of the joint, all of which are considered as Knee Osteoarthritis (KOA) with early knee degeneration. The clinical manifestations of early knee degeneration differ for each individual because of their natural progression. Even some patients have no symptoms, so clinical detection of early knee degeneration is difficult [2]. The diagnostic methods for KOA include both invasive and non-invasive computer-aided pathological diagnostic methods. Arthroscopy is the "gold standard" of invasive KOA diagnostic methods, examining the cartilage surface through fiber optic cables in order

A. Gibadullin (Ed.): ITIDMS 2021, CCIS 1703, pp. 79–92, 2022.
https://doi.org/10.1007/978-3-031-21340-3_8

to determine the treatment modality in various prognoses. This is a low-risk method for assessing knee joint. Nevertheless, this method intelligently provides an anatomical image of the articular cartilage, which cannot complete the description of cartilage function [3] and is limited in the early detection of cartilage pathology [4]. X-rays, Computed Tomography (CT) and Magnetic Resonance Imaging (MRI) are imaging based non-invasive KOA diagnostic methods, with X-rays and CT being more suitable for the diagnosis of severe or advanced KOA. MRI is suitable for diagnosing early and mid-stage knee degeneration, but the expensive diagnostic equipment and the high cost of a single test for the patient limit the availability of this chronic condition for realistic clinical diagnosis. The vibroarthrographic (VAG) signal-based knee pathology screening method is a non-invasive KOA pathology diagnostic technique with convenient and straightforward equipment operation. It does not require complex surgery, which is low cost and suitable for repeated testing, thus receiving wide attention and research in KOA clinical diagnosis.

The vibroarthrographic (VAG) signal generated during knee flexion and extension is thought to be related to pathological states of the knee joint, such as degeneration of the cartilage surface [1, 5]. The vibration generated by friction on the surface of the degenerating cartilage joint is thought to be different from those of the normal knee joint [6], which could provide useful indicators for assessing the state of articular cartilage surface roughness, softening, rupture or lubrication [7–9]. Knee vibration (VAG) signals acquired externally contain valid parameters of KOA degeneration status [10–12], which can be used as a computer-aided analysis tool to achieve non-invasive diagnosis of KOA through proper signal acquisition and processing methods. At present, it has attracted research from many scholars and achieved some research results. As early as 1929, C F Walters [13] proposed the technique of joint auscultation, which laid the foundation for knee injury detection based on signals collected from the knee joint. In 1933 Erb first reported the measurement of knee joint signals [14]. Since then, many researchers have conducted analytical studies on VAG signals in order to achieve non-invasive knee pathology diagnosis [2, 15–18]. However, it is difficult for common signal processing techniques to achieve high-precision pathological classification of VAG signals, so the auscultation signal, although useful and reliable, has not been widely used in clinical diagnosis of knee pathology [19]. Hence, improving the accuracy of pathological classification is still the focus of current research. The VAG signal is similar to other sensor acquisition signals in terms of high noise and system instability during the long-time use [20], resulting in redundant information in the acquired signal, which leads to errors in subsequent signal analysis.

In this paper, we start from the aspect of signal accuracy to optimize the results of pathology classification. In order to improve the accuracy and reliability of VAG signal acquisition, we propose a multi-channel signal fusion method to highlight the trend characteristics of the VAG target signal. However, the multi-channel signal fusion method requires priori knowledge of the target signal, and since the VAG signal is a non-stationary signal [21], it is difficult to obtain its prior information. Therefore, this paper proposes a KOA pathology diagnosis method using multi-channel VAG signal fusion, which utilizes the consistent and adaptive weighted signal fusion algorithm, so that it can achieve information fusion under the condition of minimum channel noise variance with unknown a priori knowledge. Then, together with the time-domain feature extraction and random forest feature classification methods, it can effectively improve the KOA pathology classification accuracy.

2 VAG Signal Fusion Algorithm Based on Consistency Metric and Adaptive Weights

2.1 Mathematical Model of Multi-channel Signal Fusion

Suppose X_i and X_j are the measured values of two different channels i, j. The mathematical model is conducted:

$$\begin{cases} X_i = X + n_i \\ X_j = X + n_j \end{cases} \tag{1}$$

where, X is the true value of target signal, n_i and n_j are the measurement error of different channels, which are white noise and are not correlated with X. The covariance matrix of the measured values is:

$$\begin{cases} R_{ij} = E[X_iX_j] = E[X^2] \\ R_{jj} = E[X_jX_j] = E[X^2] + E[n_j^2] \end{cases} \tag{2}$$

Then the variance σ_j^2 of the j-th channel noise is:

$$\sigma_j^2 = E[n_j^2] = R_{jj} - R_{ij} \tag{3}$$

The following solves for R_{ij}, R_{jj}:

The estimated value of R_{ij}, R_{jj} corresponding to the sampling point k for different channel measurements is denoted by $R_{ij}(k)$, $R_{ij}(k)$:

$$\begin{cases} R_{ij}(k) = \dfrac{1}{k}\sum_{m=1}^{k} X_i(m)X_j(m) \\ R_{jj}(k) = \dfrac{1}{k}\sum_{m=1}^{k} X_j(m)X_j(m) \end{cases} \tag{4}$$

According to Eq. (3), we can obtain:

$$\sigma_j^2(k) = R_{jj}(k) - R_{ij}(k) \tag{5}$$

2.2 Multi-channel Signal Consistency Metric

To achieve blind fusion with multi-channel signals, a supporting degree-based fusion method is used to implement a signal fusion method that does not depend on prior knowledge in multi-channel. According to model (1), it is assumed that the observed values of i channel at k moment on the target X are modeled as:

$$X_i(k) = X + n_i(k) \quad i = 1, 2, \cdots, N \tag{6}$$

where $X_i(k)$ is the observed value of the i-th channel at the moment k, with a total of N channels. X is the observed target, $n_i(k)$ is the observed noise at the moment k, and both $E[n_i]$ and $D[n_i]$ are unknown.

If the difference between $X_i(k)$ and $X_j(k)$ is large, it indicates that the observed values of these two channels have low mutual support. On the contrary, it indicates that the observed values of the two channels have high mutual support. In order to quantify the support degree between the observed values of each channel at the same moment, the exponential decay function quantity is introduced, which can smoothly describe the support degree of different magnitudes and avoid the absoluteness of the quantified results.

The support degree of channel i and channel j observed values at moment k is:

$$r_{ij} = \exp\left\{-\tau\left[X_i(k) - X_j(k)\right]^2\right\} \tag{7}$$

where, τ is an adjustable parameter. By adjusting the value of the parameter τ, the support metric scales for different scenes are established.

From Eq. (7), the support matrix among channels at moment k is obtained:

$$G_n = \begin{bmatrix} 1 & r_{12} & \cdots & r_{1n} \\ r_{21} & 1 & \cdots & r_{2n} \\ \vdots & \vdots & \vdots & \vdots \\ r_{n1} & r_{n2} & \cdots & 1 \end{bmatrix} \tag{8}$$

For the element of the i-th row in the support matrix, if $\sum_{j=1}^{n} r_{ij}(k)$ is large, it indicates that the observed value of the i-th channel at moment k is consistent with the majority of other channels. Conversely, the observed value of the i-th channel deviates from the majority other channels.

To reflect the integrated support degree of X_j by the other n-1 channel observed values, we define a integrated support function s_i:

$$s_i = \sum_{i=1, j\neq i}^{n} r_{ij} \quad i = 1, 2, \cdots, N \tag{9}$$

where, s_i indicates the degree of integrated support for X_j by other channels.

Definition 1. The consistency metric between the i-th channel observed values and the other $n - 1$ channel observed values at moment k is:

$$\xi_i(k) = \frac{s_i}{n-1} \quad i = 1, 2, \cdots, N \tag{10}$$

where obviously $0 < \xi_i(k) \le 1$. $\xi_i(k)$ can reflect the closeness between the observed value of the i-th channel and other sensors at a certain observation moment.

In order to consider the robust information contained in the channels at different moments, the consistency metric at different moments is proposed.

Definition 2: At the moment k, the mean value of the consistency in the i-th channel is denoted as $\overline{\xi_i(k)}$:

$$\overline{\xi_i(k)} = \begin{cases} \xi_i(1) & k = 1 \\ \frac{k-1}{k}\overline{\xi_{i-1}(k)} + \frac{1}{k}\xi_i(k) & k > 1 \end{cases} \tag{11}$$

2.3 Adaptive Weighting Factor Correction

In order to consider that the measurement variance is influenced by various factors such as the credibility of the sensor itself at acquisition, environmental disturbances and so on, and to reduce the deviation between the estimated and true values, an adaptive weighting algorithm is proposed to change the influence degree of the observed value variance among individual channels on the weighting coefficients. This method can solve the problem of optimal assignment of weights when multi-channel estimation to the same target parameter, ensure the reliability of weighted fusion results and minimize the total variance of measurement after multi-channel signal fusion, so that the signal fusion results have a minimal error with the true value.

Based on the model (1), the mathematical model of the observed value in the i-th channel at the moment k can be expressed as:

$$X_i(k) = X(k) + n_i(k) \quad i = 1, 2, \cdots, N \tag{12}$$

where $X(k)$ is the real signal, $n_i(k)$ is the white noise, and its variance is $\sigma_i^2 = E[n_i^2(k)]$.

Assuming that the observations of the target by different channels are non-interfering with each other, the estimate of X can be expressed as $\hat{X}$:

$$\hat{X} = \sum_{i=1}^{N} W_i X_i \tag{13}$$

where W_i is weighting coefficient and $\sum_{i=1}^{N} W_i = 1$.

The estimated variance is:

$$\hat{\sigma}^2 = \sum_{i=1}^{N} W_i^2 \sigma_i^2 \tag{14}$$

where, σ_i^2 is the noise variance in the i-th channel.

To minimize the total variance in Eq. (14), construct the auxiliary function as following:

$$f(W_1, W_2, \cdots, W_N, \lambda) = \sum_{i=1}^{N} W_i^2 \sigma_i^2 + \lambda \left(\sum_{i=1}^{N} W_i - 1 \right) \tag{15}$$

Then the minimum problem under condition $\sum_{i=1}^{N} W_i = 1$ can be equated to the conditional extremum problem:

$$\begin{cases} \frac{\partial f}{\partial W_1} = 2W_1 \sigma_1^2 + \lambda = 0 \\ \frac{\partial f}{\partial W_2} = 2W_2 \sigma_2^2 + \lambda = 0 \\ \cdots \\ \frac{\partial f}{\partial W_N} = 2W_N \sigma_N^2 + \lambda = 0 \\ \sum_{i=1}^{N} W_i - 1 = 0 \end{cases} \tag{16}$$

i.e.,

$$\begin{cases} W_i = \frac{u}{\sigma_i^2}, i = 1, 2, \cdots, n, u = -\frac{\lambda}{2} \\ W_1 + W_2 + \cdots + W_N = 1 \end{cases} \tag{17}$$

The solution is:

$$u = \frac{1}{\sum_{i=1}^{N} \frac{1}{\sigma_i^2}} \tag{18}$$

Taking Eq. (18) into $W_j = \frac{u}{\sigma_j^2}, j = 1, 2, \cdots, N$, we can obtain the weight coefficient W_j for the j-th channel:

$$W_j = \frac{1}{\sigma_j^2 \sum_{i=1}^{N} \frac{1}{\sigma_i^2}}, j = 1, 2, \cdots, N \tag{19}$$

W_j is the weight allocation value of each channel under the condition of minimum total variance, which is related to the variance of each channel. The optimal weights W_j for each channel can be calculated according to Eq. (5):

$$W_j = \frac{1}{\frac{1}{k} \sum_{m=1}^{k} \sum_{m=1}^{k} \left[X_j(m) X_j(m) - X_i(m) X_j(m) \right] \sum_{i=1}^{N} \frac{1}{\sigma_i^2}} \quad j, i = 1, 2, \cdots, N \tag{20}$$

Signal fusion algorithm based on consistency metric and adaptive weighting.

For multi-channel signal fusion, based on the mathematical model of Eq. (1), in order to make full use of the multi-channel observed value with high consistency and reliability at sampling k, according to Definition 2, the consistency of the j-th channel at sampling k can be obtained as:

$$\overline{\xi_j(k)} = \begin{cases} \xi_j(1) & k = 1 \\ \frac{k-1}{k}\overline{\xi_{j-1}(k)} + \frac{1}{k}\xi_j(k) & k > 1 \end{cases} \qquad (21)$$

In order to improve the signal fusion accuracy, considering the minimum noise variance of the observed values, an improved adaptive weighting coefficient is proposed based on Eq. (20). With channel consistency:

$$\begin{cases} v_j(k) = W_j\overline{\xi_j(k)} \\ W_j = \dfrac{1}{\frac{1}{k}\sum\limits_{m=1}^{k}\sum\limits_{m=1}^{k}[X_j(m)X_j(m)-X_i(m)X_j(m)]\sum\limits_{i=1}^{N}\frac{1}{\sigma_i^2}} \end{cases} \quad j, i = 1, 2, \cdots, N \qquad (22)$$

The signal fusion based on multi-channel consistency and adaptive weighting coefficient is estimated as $\tilde{X}(k)$:

$$\tilde{X}(k) = \frac{\sum\limits_{i=1}^{N}[v_i(k)X_i(k)]}{\sum\limits_{i=1}^{N}v_i(k)} \quad i = 1, 2, \cdots, N \qquad (23)$$

3   KOA Pathology Screening Algorithm Based on Consistency and Adaptive Weighted Signal Fusion

In order to improve the screening accuracy of the KOA pathology screening algorithm, this paper proposes a KOA pathology screening algorithm based on consistency and adaptive weighted signal fusion. Since each collected VAG data is the signal of the subject squatting three times at a uniform speed, the VAG signal was first split into 3-channel data. Then the information of the multi-channel data was fused into a group of VAG signals based on consistency and adaptive weighted signal fusion algorithms, followed by the extraction of 11 time-domain features of the VAG signals, and finally, the random forest was used to classify the features to achieve KOA pathological screening. The flow chart of the algorithm is shown in Fig. 1.

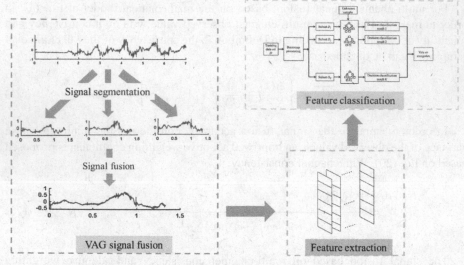

Fig. 1. The frame of algorithm.

Feature extraction and classification are performed on the VAG fusion signal to achieve knee joint pathological screening. Firstly, 11 time-domain feature parameters of the VAG signal are extracted as follows (Table 1):

Table 1. The expression of 11 time-domain feature parameters.

Feature expression	Feature expression	Feature expression
$TF_1 = \left(\frac{1}{N} \sum\limits_{n=1}^{N} x^2(n) \right)^{1/2}$	$TF_2 = \|x_{\max}(n)\| - \|x_{\min}(n)\|$	$TF_3 = \frac{1}{N} \sum\limits_{n=1}^{N} x(n)$
$TF_4 = \frac{1}{N} \sum\limits_{n=1}^{N} (x(n) - TF_3)^2$	$TF_5 = X_P / \left\| \frac{1}{N} \sum\limits_{n=1}^{N} \sqrt{\|x(n)\|} \right\|^2$	$TF_6 = \frac{1}{N} \sum\limits_{n=1}^{N} \left(\frac{x(n) - TF_3}{\sqrt{TF_4}} \right)^4$
$TF_7 = \dfrac{\frac{1}{N} \sum\limits_{n=1}^{N} (\|x(n)\| - TF_3)^3}{TF_1^3}$	$TF_8 = \dfrac{X_P}{\|TF_3\|}$	$TF_9 = \dfrac{m_{x'}}{m_x} = \dfrac{\sigma_{x'}/\sigma_{x'}}{\sigma_{x'}/\sigma_x}$ d

Note: $x(n)$ represents the discrete time series. X_p indicates the peak of signal. m_x denotes the square root of the ratio of the variance of the first derivative $\sigma_{x'}$ of the signal to the variance d of the original signal σ_x, x'' represents the second derivative of the signal.

TF_{10} [22] is the variance of the mean-squared value, which calculates the mean square value of the VAG signal in a fixed duration period, and then calculates the variance of the entire signal.

TF_{11} [23] is the turn count, which is to calculate the number of signal inflection points greater than a certain threshold.

The random forest classifier [24] is an integrated classifier proposed by Leo Breiman et al. It consists of several decision trees and the final classification result is decided by an integrated vote of the decision tree classification results. It has fast training speed, high classification accuracy, and good tolerance to outliers and noise. Moreover, as its classification results are not easily overfitted, it has wide applications in medical, bioinformatics, and management fields.

We extracted 11 time-domain features of all VAG signals and input them into a random forest classifier to achieve KOA pathology screening.

We use accuracy, precision, and specificity to evaluate the classification results and compare the effects:

$$accuracy = \frac{TP + TN}{TP + FN + TN + FP} \tag{24}$$

$$precision = \frac{TP}{TP + FP} \tag{25}$$

$$specificity = \frac{TN}{TN + FP} \tag{26}$$

where, TP is true positive, TN is true negative, FP is false positive and FN is false negative.

4   Experimental Results and Discussion

Based on all the collected signals were generated by the subjects performing three uniform squatting movements, firstly, they were segmented into three segments to obtain three channels of VAG signals. Figure 2 is a raw VAG signal. In Fig. 3, $X1$, $X2$, $X3$ are segmented 3-channel signals. Figure 3 shows the fusion signal X_fusion.

4.1   VAG Signal Multi-channel Signal Fusion Results

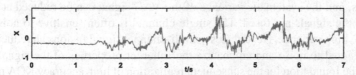

Fig. 2. The raw VAG signal.

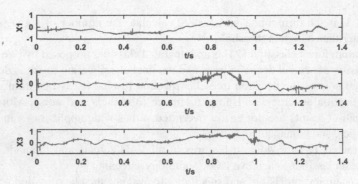

Fig. 3. VAG segmentation signal of 3-channel.

X1, X2, X3 are the three segmented signals of the raw signal X.

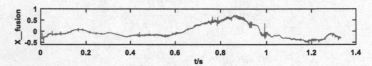

Fig. 4. The fusion signal.

Figure 3 shows the fusion results of the 3-channel signals. It can be seen that the VAG multi-channel signal fusion method proposed in this paper not only retains the signal trend intact, but also effectively reduces the channel bias. For example, there is not an apparent VAG signal trend of $X3$ in Fig. 3, but the VAG signal trend is effectively enhanced in the fused signal, as shown in Fig. 4. This is because the method proposed in this paper considers the degree of similarity among channels by constructing a support matrix to maximally eliminate unreasonable information and retain the weight of reasonably useful information. And the method proposed in this paper can adaptively change the weights of channels, when a channel signal is noisier, the weight value of it will be reduced, and the weights of other channels will be increased accordingly, so that the more components of the target signal can be retained in the fused signal. The noise variance minimization condition is considered when deducing the adaptive weighting coefficients, and the systematic variance of the VAG signal can be reduced at the same time when the signals are fused. The single-channel is often sensitive to noise, which could cause high variance. Nevertheless, multi-channel signal fusion can reduce the sensitivity of signal to noise and emphasize the inherent properties of the signal, both of which lay the foundation for the subsequent realization of high accuracy KOA pathology diagnosis.

4.2   VAG Signal Pathology Screening Result

In this paper, 487 sets of VAG data have been experimented, among which there were 254 normal VAG signals and 233 abnormal (KOA) VAG signals. The experimental dataset was obtained by orthopaedic surgeons of Xi'an Fourth Military Medical University, using acceleration sensors to collect signals from the patient's knee joint, which was used for research experiments. As in Sect. 3, 11 time-domain features of the multi-channel fused VAG signal are extracted, and time-domain features are fed into the random forest classifier to achieve pathological classification of the VAG signal. Table 2 and Table 3 compare the pathology classification results before and after signal fusion. To contrast the classification effects of the classifiers, the random forest classification results are compared with the K-NN and SVM classifiers.

Table 2.   The classification result of raw VAG signal.

Classifier used		K-NN		SVM		Random forest	
Confusion matrix		Predict value		Predict value		Predict value	
		Positive	Negative	Positive	Negative	Positive	Negative
Actual value	Positive	49	6	45	6	42	2
	Negative	4	39	19	28	8	46
Accuracy		0.90		0.74		0.90	
Precision		0.90		0.76		0.91	
Specificity		0.90		0.60		0.85	

Table 3.   The classification results of the fusion VAG signal.

Classifier used		K-NN		SVM		Random forest	
Confusion matrix		Predict value		Predict value		Predict value	
		Positive	Negative	Positive	Negative	Positive	Negative
Actual value	Positive	41	1	46	10	46	3
	Negative	5	50	7	34	2	46
Accuracy		0.94		0.82		0.95	
Precision		0.94		0.83		0.95	
Specificity		0.91		0.83		0.96	

It can be seen from Table 2 and Table 3 that, in general, K-NN, SVM and random forest after signal fusion all outperform the results without optimization, in which K-NN improves the accuracy by 4%, SVM improves the specificity by 23%, and random forest improves the specificity by 11%. In particular, the multi-channel signal fusion improves the classification results of SVM the most. It shows that the multi-channel signal fusion method proposed in this paper provides advantages in analysing and processing VAG signals. The method based on consistency and adaptive weighted signal fusion proposed in this paper achieves blind reconstruction of non-smooth signals by weighted fusion after target signal segmentation. Moreover, this method does not need to consider the prior knowledge of the signal, and can adaptively enhance the proportion of true VAG signals in the acquired signal, so that the originally obscure VAG signals are more obvious in the signal after fusion, which makes the extracted features have greater inter-class differentiation and provide better performance on classifiers. As shown in Table 3, the fused signals obtained by our method can improve the pathological screening ability at the same amount of original data. However, the limitation of this signal fusion method is that the algorithm requires multi-channel acquiring signals. In this paper, multiple channel acquisition is simulated by signal segmentation. If the alignment of signals in each channel at the knee flexion moment is more standard, the signal fusion effect is better. Otherwise, if there is a deviation in the alignment at the knee flexion moment, the signal fusion result will produce error.

Both Table 2 and Table 3 compare the classification ability of random forest with SVM and K-NN. Before signal fusion, the classification results of random forest and K-NN are similar, where the accuracy both are 0.90, and they are better than SVM, which is 0.74. The precision of random forest is higher than that of K-NN, values are 0.91 and 0.90 respectively, and the specificity of K-NN is higher than random forest, they are 0.90 and 0.85, respectively. For the same case after signal fusion, random forest has the best classification result with 0.95 for accuracy, 0.95 for precision and 0.96 for specificity, which is a significant improvement over the classification result before fusion. The K-NN classification results also improved, but the classification results are not as good as random forest, with accuracy, precision, and specificity of 0.94, 0.94 and 0.91, respectively. Signal fusion has the greatest effect on the SVM classifier, with accuracy improving from 0.74 to 0.82, precision improving from 0.76 to 0.83, and specificity improving from 0.60 to 0.83, with maximum optimization of 23% in the classification results. In general, the best classifier is the random forest, especially after signal fusion specificity can reach 0.96.

Table 4. Performance of our method and other methods.

	Accuracy	Precision	Specificity
Kim K S et al. (2009) [19]	0.91	0.93	0.92
Rangayyan, R. M. and Y. Wu (2010)	0.78	–	0.82
Wu Y et al. (2013)	0.87	–	–
Sharma M et al. (2018)	0.90	0.84	0.89
Rui GONG et al. (2020)	0.87	–	–
Shidore, Mrunal M et al. (2021)	0.89	0.90	0.91
Proposed method	0.95	0.95	0.96

Table 4 compares this paper's VAG pathology diagnosis results and other methods. It can be seen that the proposed method has great advantages in terms of accuracy, precision, and specificity. The experiment proves that the KOA pathology screening method based on multi-channel signal fusion proposed in this paper can effectively improve the pathology screening rate and achieve highly accurate KOA pathology screening.

5 Conclusion

In this paper, we propose a VAG signal fusion method based on consistency metric and adaptive weighting to improve the diagnosis rate of KOA pathology. For the first time, we propose the idea of multi-channel signal fusion, which uses consistency metric to take into account the mutual support degree between channel signals and enhance the consistency of channel information. Adaptive weighting can change the impact of the noise variance among each channel signal on the weight coefficients, ensuring the minimum total variance of the fused signals and achieving adaptive weight assignment. Then the multi-channel signals are fused according to the weighting coefficients. This method gets rid of the reliance on prior knowledge, realizes the adaptive weighted fusion of non-stationary VAG signals under the situation that prior information is difficult to obtain, improves the error tolerance in the signal fusion process. The reconstructed VAG fusion signal makes the observed signal of the sensor closer to the true VAG signal, improves the reliability of the VAG signal, and is more beneficial to later analyse the characteristics of non-stationary VAG signals. Finally, we design a KOA pathology screening method using multi-channel signal fusion. This method extracts 11 time-domain features from the fused VAG signal, and feeds the signal features into random forest classifier with accuracy, precision, and specificity of 0.95, 0.95, 0.96, respectively. The experimental results demonstrate that the proposed method obtains a high correct classification rate and could provide an effective non-invasive computational aid for the clinical diagnosis of KOA pathology.

Acknowledgments. This research was supported by the Key Research and Development Program of Shaanxi Province, No. D5140200023.

References

1. McCoy, G.F., McCrea, J.D., Beverland, D.E., Kernohan, W.G., Mollan, R.A.: Vibration arthrography as a diagnostic aid in diseases of the knee. A preliminary report. J. Bone Joint Surg. **69**(2), 288–293 (1987). British volume
2. Rangayyan, R.M., Wu, Y.F.: Screening of knee-joint vibroarthrographic signals using statistical parameters and radial basis functions. Med. Biol. Eng. Compu. **46**(3), 223–232 (2008)
3. Van Breuseghem, I.: Ultrastructural MR imaging techniques of the knee articular cartilage: problems for routine clinical application. Eur. Radiol. **14**(2), 184–192 (2004)
4. Jiang, C.C., Lee, J.H., Yuan, T.T.: Vibration arthrometry in the patients with failed total knee replacement. IEEE Trans. Biomed. Eng. **47**(2), 219–227 (2000)

5. Frank, C.B., Rangayyan, R.M., Bell, G.D.: Analysis of knee joint sound signals for non-invasive diagnosis of cartilage pathology. IEEE Eng. Med. Biol. Mag. **9**(1), 65–68 (1990)
6. Krishnan, S., Rangayyan, R.M., Bell, G.D., Frank, C.B.: Adaptive time-frequency analysis of knee joint vibroarthrographic signals for noninvasive screening of articular cartilage pathology. IEEE Trans. Biomed. Eng. **47**(6), 773–783 (2000)
7. Bircher, E.: Zur diagnose der meniscusluxation und des meniscusabrisses. Zentralbl f. Chir **40**, 1852 (1913)
8. Blodgett, W.E.: Auscultation of the knee joint. Boston Med. Surg. J. **146**(3), 63–66 (1902)
9. Peylan, A.: Direct auscultation of the joints; preliminary clinical observations. Rheumatism **9**(4), 77–81 (1953)
10. Steindler, A.: Auscultation of joints. JBJS **19**(1), 121–136 (1937)
11. Szabo, E., Danis, L., Torok, Z.: Examination of the acoustic phenomena observed in the knee. Traumatologia **15**(2), 118–127 (1972)
12. Chu, M.L., Gradisar, I.A., Zavodney, L.D.: Possible clinical application of a noninvasive monitoring technique of cartilage damage in pathological knee joints. J. Clin. Eng. **3**(1), 19–27 (1978)
13. Walters, C.F.: The value of joint auscultation. The Lancet **213**(5514), 920–921 (1929)
14. Erb, K.H.: Über die möglichkeit der registrierung von gelenkgeräuschen. Langenbeck's Arch. Surg. **241**(11), 237–245 (1933)
15. Rangayyan, R.M., Wu, Y.: Screening of knee-joint vibroarthrographic signals using probability density functions estimated with Parzen windows. Biomed. Signal Process. Control **5**(1), 53–58 (2010)
16. Wu, Y., et al.: Quantification of knee vibroarthrographic signal irregularity associated with patellofemoral joint cartilage pathology based on entropy and envelope amplitude measures. Comput. Methods Programs Biomed. **130**, 1–12 (2016)
17. Chen, J.C., Tung, P.C., Huang, S.F., Wu, S.W., Lin, S.L., Tu, K.L.: Extraction and screening of knee joint vibroarthrographic signals using the empirical mode decomposition method. Int. J. Innov. Comput. Inf. Control **9**(6), 2689–2700 (2013)
18. Shidore, M.M., Athreya, S.S., Deshpande, S., Jalnekar, R.: Screening of knee-joint vibroarthrographic signals using time and spectral domain features. Biomed. Signal Process. Control **68**, 102808 (2021)
19. Kim, K.S., Seo, J.H., Kang, J.U., Song, C.G.: An enhanced algorithm for knee joint sound classification using feature extraction based on time-frequency analysis. Comput. Methods Programs Biomed. **94**(2), 198–206 (2009)
20. Chang, H., Xue, L., Qin, W., Yuan, G., Yuan, W.: An integrated MEMS gyroscope array with higher accuracy output. Sensors **8**(4), 2886–2899 (2008)
21. Sharma, M., Acharya, U.R.: Analysis of knee-joint vibroarthographic signals using bandwidth-duration localized three-channel filter bank. Comput. Electr. Eng. **72**, 191–202 (2018)
22. Rangayyan, R.M., Wu, Y.: Analysis of vibroarthrographic signals with features related to signal variability and radial-basis functions. Ann. Biomed. Eng. **37**(1), 156–163 (2009)
23. Willison, R.G.: Analysis of electrical activity in healthy and dystrophic muscle in man. J. Neurol. Neurosurg. Psychiatry **27**(5), 386 (1964)
24. Breiman, L.: Random forests. Mach. Learn. **45**(1), 5–32 (2001)
25. Wu, Y., Cai, S., Yang, S., Zheng, F., Xiang, N.: Classification of knee joint vibration signals using bivariate feature distribution estimation and maximal posterior probability decision criterion. Entropy **15**(4), 1375–1387 (2013)
26. Gong, R., Hase, K., Goto, H., Yoshioka, K., Ota, S.: Knee osteoarthritis detection based on the combination of empirical mode decomposition and wavelet analysis. J. Biomech. Sci. Eng. **15**(3), 20-00017 (2020)

Prioritization of Distributed Worker Processes Based on Etcd Locks

Teymur Zeynally[1]([✉]) [iD], Dmitry Demidov[1] [iD], and Lubomir Dimitrov[2] [iD]

[1] Moscow Polytechnic University, Moscow, Russian Federation
z.teymur.e@gmail.com, d.g.demidov@mospolytech.ru
[2] Technical University of Sofia, Sofia, Bulgaria
lubomir_dimitrov@tu-sofia.bg

Abstract. This paper describes the prioritization of iterative processes in corporate information systems. The processes are distributed, and each node is a peer. The nodes coordinate their actions through the etcd replicated key-vale store. The nodes are synchronized over NTP and iterate at certain points in time. The paper outlines the main ways of setting priorities. The general points and problems that the proposed prioritization mechanism solves are described. The basic principle on which the proposed mechanism is based is described. Requirements are imposed on the speed of the order determination operation. An algorithm for determining the order and calculating priorities is described. The process of obtaining information from indicators and other nodes with subsequent aggregation is described. The problems of determining the order, taking the lock are described and a solution to these problems is proposed. The main points of the prioritization mechanism are schematically depicted. The destabilizing factors and the reaction of the system to them are discussed.

Keywords: Distributed system · Worker process · Key-value storage · Etcd · Prioritization

1 Introduction

Today, in corporate information systems, worker processes and widely used to solve a wide range of tasks. In this work, a worker process is understood as an iterative process that executes a certain block of code according to a schedule. Schedules can be quite flexible and depend on the current load on the system. Examples of worker process payloads include parsing queues, sending notifications, processing data, and so on.

With the development of corporate information systems, the performance of a single instance of the application becomes insufficient to complete the tasks and ensure their continuity. Under these conditions, they resort to horizontal scaling of systems: they deploy instances of the application process on several computing nodes [1].

In horizontally scaled systems, it becomes necessary to synchronize or coordinate iterations of worker processes. This need arises when the simultaneous execution of the worker process is unacceptable, and in a horizontally scaled system it is difficult to

A. Gibadullin (Ed.): ITIDMS 2021, CCIS 1703, pp. 93–103, 2022.
https://doi.org/10.1007/978-3-031-21340-3_9

ensure this. An example of such a need is sending notifications (for example, by email) or copying files: it is unacceptable for the same notification to be sent several times or file copying to start at the same time. In such cases, resort to the use of, for example, queues. However, the basis for current work is to solve this problem through distributed blockers or key-value stores. The essence of this solution is to capture the lock for the iteration and release it at the end.

In the current work, systems of workers are considered, which independently of each other have reliable information about the point in time at which iteration should be started. The time on the nodes is synchronized via NTP [5]. At the point of iteration, the nodes start to acquire the lock. The node that has acquired the lock performs an iteration, informs the rest of the nodes about its success, and the whole system goes into waiting for the moment for the next iteration. These restrictions may seem exotic and of little use in practice, however, the given restrictions are the behavior of a peer-to-peer distributed system of worker processes, coordinating their actions through a key-value blocker or other concurrency control method in distributed systems [10]. This behavior is typical for systems in which there is no leader selection for further coordination of iterations, each node is independent. In order to provide one iteration in a certain period of time, each node can calculate the iteration moments according to a given schedule and, thus, iterate at the same time with the rest of the nodes.

In such systems, failures and delays are possible, which are caused by various factors. For example, on certain nodes, a particular type of iteration may always fail due to infrastructure issues. Or some node is overloaded with other tasks. There are many such scenarios, and the logical solution is to prioritize the nodes of the system depending on these factors. This kind of prioritization will increase the performance of the system as a whole. This paper describes how to implement the prioritization of peer-to-peer worker processes in a given restrictions in practice.

2   Materials and Methods

The methodological basis of the current study is the analysis of the mechanism for prioritizing worker processes in corporate information systems and existing software systems. The current study also analyzes common approaches. As a result of the analysis, a mechanism for prioritizing peer-to-peer distributed worker processes is proposed. In addition, the study suggests a practical implementation of the described mechanism based on the etcd storage. For practical implementation, etcd version 3.5 was used. The logic for interacting with etcd described in this paper was developed on net6.0.

3   Results

3.1   Review of Existing Approaches and Solutions

If we consider dotnet solutions in this area, then the currently most popular Quartz and Hangfire solutions work on the principle of one coordinating node, which forms a queue of tasks executed on cluster nodes [11, 11]. This approach is fundamentally different from the one described in the introduction and which will be discussed further.

In addition, they basically use SQL servers, which are harder to maintain, replicate, and require much more computing resources than lightweight key-value stores [2].

The organization of prioritization through a priority queue is the most common method used for a wide range of tasks and many practical solutions for the entire industry. There are a number of algorithms for organizing such a queue, and relational DBMS provide their own functionality to achieve the desired behavior. However, in relation to the problem of prioritization of distributed worker processes, one can omit the need to select a leader and coordinate tasks through him by means of a queue. In cases where each node, being part of the system, has the same rights and information as all other nodes, the approach to queuing is different from the generally accepted ones. In this work, it will be with the specifics of key-value storages.

3.2 Choosing a Key-Value Store

Currently, there are three main, most popular key-value stores: etcd, Apache ZooKeeper, HashiCorp Consul. Also, there is Redis, it is faster, but it is more suitable for caching, due to its asynchronous replication. When it is required to trust the fault tolerance of a key-value store, asynchronous replication is not acceptable [6].

In terms of functionality, each of the three key-value repositories has approximately the same set of tools. However, etcd has several advantages. Interaction with etcd can be organized through gRPC, which allows you to generate a client codebase for most modern languages, as well as gRPC message passing faster than REST due to the smaller message size [8]. Whereas ZooKeeper has its own Jute RPC protocol [14].

Etcd and Consul, although similar in functionality, solve different problems. Etcd is better suited for the role of distributed consistent key-value storage, because Consul does not support multiversioned keys, conditional transactions, or reliable streaming event subscriptions. However, for end-to-end cluster service discovery, Consul is better suited [14].

Considering all of the above, etcd was chosen, however, it is clear that etcd does not have a cardinal advantage over other key-value stores. At the same time, everything that is described in the current article can be adapted to other key-value stores.

3.3 Organization of Data Considering the Specifics of using Key-Value Storages

Before describing the use of key-value stores to solve the current problem, it is necessary to describe what operations key-value stores can perform. There are not many of them: adding a key, an atomic comparison operation with a replacement, getting a value by a key, getting a range of keys by a prefix, deleting a key [4]. All of the listed operations, except for range operations, are performed in $O(1)$. Also, the keys are equipped with TTL (time to live) and are deleted from the storage when the TTL expires [4]. Some of stores allow you to monitor key value changes. Such stores are well suited for distributed locks, and some of them provide out-of-the-box mechanisms for the Mutex primitive. Key-value stores do not provide out-of-the-box prioritization mechanisms, but by manipulating the provided operations, a complex data structure can be organized and interacted with [4].

In order to determine the contents of the repository, it is necessary to understand what information the nodes need and what they will do with it.

Prioritization assumes that the node or worker of the process will have some kind of priority. The priority of a node depends on the load on the node itself. This priority can be calculated from the load on the hardware. Priority can be given to a specific worker process for a specific node. It depends on the success of this node iterations over the given process. This priority can be calculated based on the execution history of concrete process on concrete node. However, how is this priority measured? There are not many answers to this question. There is an enumeration approach when there are few priorities. Conventionally: high, medium, low. There is an approach when the priority is set by a non-negative number, and the smaller number has the higher priority. With this approach, the maximum priority is 0, and the minimum is limited by the data type. In the current work, it was decided not to be tied to an enumerated priority, but to take a more general approach, limiting ourselves to the byte type [0.0.255].

Now more about what information the nodes need. All interaction takes place between the nodes of the non-Byzantine system: the nodes will not intentionally distort information [7, 7]. Therefore, each node can report its own priority, and the other nodes will not question this value. At the same time, knowing the priority values of all nodes, a particular node can determine its order in this virtual queue.

Keys can take arbitrary values, up to hierarchical structures, such as JSON, which can store priorities for all nodes. However, this option is not suitable due to the fact that the nodes will have to synchronize in order to access the resource to mutate the value. Moreover, nodes can log out or reboot with a new ID, the structure will only grow. This approach is unacceptable and contradicts the concept of key-value stores.

Thus, the name of the priority key is determined by the following expression: "{Service Name}/Priority/{Process ID}/{Node ID}". For example, "Service1/Priority/EmailWorker/7bec08ef" $= 0$. If a node needs to get the node priorities for a particular process, you can query the storage for all keys and values in the range "{Service Name}/Priority/{Process ID}/", and if for all, then "{Service Name}/Priority/". If you need to store and get the priority of the node itself, depending on hardware resources, then similarly "{Service Name}/NodePriority/{Node ID}". If a node is down or out of the system, then, after the expiration of the TTL, information about the priority of this node will be deleted from the storage. Some key-value stores allow you to create a lease on a store. One lease is created per node. All keys created by this node are bound to lease. Accordingly, until the lease has expired TTL, all keys associated with this lease will be available in the storage. Thus, the node only needs to maintain the TTL of the lease by constantly updating it, rather than updating the TTL for each key individually.

3.4 Prioritization Algorithm

General Points. Before directly iterating the worker process, the node takes an exclusive lock on the entire system for the iteration. The node that has taken the lock starts executing the payload, the remaining nodes enter the lock wait state. At the same time, the storage itself is responsible for the waiting process, and not the client code. Etcd locks have a peculiarity: when the node holding the lock performs a lock release operation on the store, the lock will be acquired by the node that first entered the lock pending state. If the rest of the nodes started acquiring the lock at the same time, which is exactly what happens, according to the restrictions described earlier, then their order is determined by the storage itself by the time the request was received and the result of replication. The repository can also use a logical clock in terms of what happened before or what happened after [3]. Nodes waiting for a lock hold a connection to a store that will notify the node if it has acquired the lock.

Obviously, the prioritization algorithm must be executed before the lock is taken. It is also clear that to organize a virtual queue, the specifics of etcd locks should be used. By organizing a queue of nodes waiting for blocking. Accordingly, the nodes in this queue will be organized by their priorities.

There is no node in the system that coordinates blocking queues or prioritizes other nodes: each node is independent. Therefore, the nodes themselves must somehow agree on which of them and in what order takes the lock. As previously noted, the nodes themselves calculate their priority. Also, each node knows the priority of the other nodes. With this information, the node can calculate the order in which it should take the lock. However, the nodes, at the time of execution, do not have enough information about who is already waiting for the lock and at what point it is necessary to send a request to acquire the lock. Delaying a multiple of the order before acquiring the lock is obviously a bad decision. Need to somehow find out how many nodes are already holding or waiting for a lock. There is a way for etcd to request this information, however, the question is how often to request this information in case the queue does not fit and how long will this whole process be before taking the lock?

Complexity Requirements. The main requirement for the prioritization algorithm, which is executed before taking the lock, is the requirement for the speed of this algorithm. It will definitely take some time, because it is necessary to agree with the rest of the nodes on the order. At the same time, worker iterations themselves can be frequent, several iterations per second, this algorithm should not lead to system performance degradation, it is just an auxiliary mechanism. Lock acquisition is not an instant process and its duration depends on the ping to storages and on the speed of their replication (replication must be synchronous). Therefore, it is obvious that before blocking, it is not necessary to find out from all nodes their priority and to request information from the storage several times about the number of nodes that have captured or are waiting for the block at the moment. Moreover, it is fraught with collisions. However, it is imperative to provide a configurable watchdog timer, after which the entire process is interrupted regardless of the order and proceeds to lock capture. This watchdog timer's timeout should be small, about a second, and definitely larger than the ping to the storage.

Ordering and Prioritizing. To determine the order, it is proposed to use two types of priorities: node priority and worker process priority. The node priority is the overall priority for all workers on the node. It depends on the load on the node host, for example, CPU or RAM load. It is possible to register several indicators in the system, reporting the result in byte, and aggregate them in various ways. It also possible to make in the architecture the extension points for these needs. The input data for the calculation function is a byte matrix, the columns of which are the values of the indicator in a certain time interval, and the rows are the indicators themselves. The calculation function returns the priority in byte. The priority of a worker process is a measure of how successful a particular process was running on a given node. At the same time, it is the priority of the worker process that has more weight, because even on the most overloaded node in the system, the priority iteration of the worker process will be executed, unlike the nodes where it fails. The priority of a worker process can also be calculated differently. The input data for the worker process priority calculation function is an array of temporary failure points for this process execution. The calculation function returns the priority in byte. The implementation of functions with the signature described above is not important in this work. Implementations can range from simple counting or median functions to complex cognitive models.

Receiving Information from Indicators and other Nodes with Subsequent Aggregation. As noted earlier, determining the order of nodes and the place of the current node in this order should occur instantly. At the same time, each node must at this moment know exactly its priority and the priorities of other nodes in the system. Moreover, all nodes must have the same information for correct calculations.

Earlier in this paper, we have already described the principle of organizing data in a storage. However, questions remain about how to request this data, how often nodes should update this information, and how to prevent desynchronization between nodes.

For both types of priorities, the algorithm for obtaining information from the storage is the same: the node needs to request keys in a certain range. However, the result of this request is not enough, you need to receive information about updates in the specified range at the time these updates are committed to the repository. To do this, etcd allows you to establish a duplex connection to the repository and interact with it through message passing. Accordingly, a message with a request to subscribe to updates in a certain range is transmitted from the node via this channel. And at the moments when new values are fixed in the storage, the storage will send corresponding messages through this channel. There are two key points in this process.

First: between requesting the current values in the range and subscribing to new events, there may be changes in keys that will not be included in the result of the first request and will not be transmitted via the channel established after. The events themselves took place somewhere in the middle. But since etcd versions all the data in its store, each response from that store is accompanied by a 64-bit revision value. A request for a range of current values will return with that same value. When composing an event subscription request message, it is critical to pass this parameter in order for etcd to respond with all events that have occurred since revision. Thus, events will not be missed and data consistency among nodes will not be broken.

The second key point is that this connection is easily broken during network failures. It may not seem obvious, but the rest of the etcd messages that are sent without establishing a duplex connection, can be routed by the client to another storage node on failure. Or they can be resubmitted without any further action from the developer. This is provided by gRPC clients. However, with a duplex channel, this is purely technically impossible to produce at the moment. In this case, it is necessary to clear all received data and the current state, and then repeat the process of requesting actual data with resubscribing to events.

It is proposed to implement two aggregators: an aggregator for data received from all nodes, and an aggregator for data collected on the current node. Accordingly, all data on the priorities of nodes and processes received from the storage is sent to the first aggregator, and the data collected from the indicators and data on the success of the processes are sent to the second.

Data from the indicators on the node can be requested in a loop in order and updated at any time and immediately sent to the second aggregator. The second aggregator receives raw information as input. It passes the received information to the input of the above-described functions that calculate the priority, after which it updates the data in the storage.

The aggregator of data from all nodes will then be used as a data source for calculating the order of the nodes (Fig. 1).

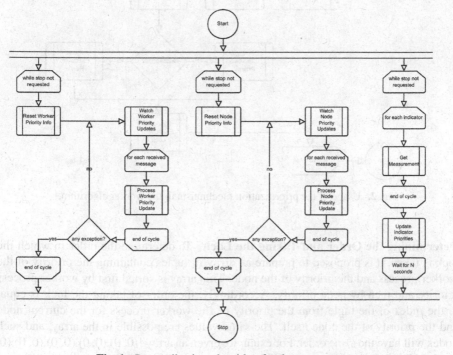

Fig. 1. Data collection algorithm for the aggregators.

Interaction Interface with Locks for the Worker Process. Interaction with the prioritization mechanism from the worker process is proposed to be organized through three functions: wait for the queue, reset the priority, lower the priority. The main function is the function of waiting for the queue before taking the lock, it is the key one in this paper and its logic will be described later. The reset and downgrade functions execute before the lock is released, which means that they should not delay the release of the lock. They tell the current node information aggregator about new inputs, and it performs the appropriate actions with the execution history and updates the priority in the storage (Fig. 2).

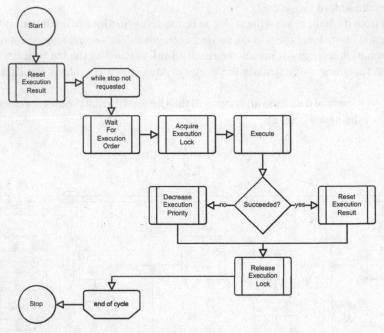

Fig. 2. Usage of the prioritization mechanism in the worker algorithm.

Determining the Order and Taking the Lock. To determine the order in which the lock is taken, it is proposed to prepare an array of tuples containing the priority of the worker process and the priority of the node. This array is sorted first by worker process priority and then by node priority. Accordingly, the order of taking the lock is equal to the index of the tuple from the priority of the worker process for the current node and the priority of the node itself. The same values are possible in the array, and such nodes will have the same order. For example, given an array [(0, 0),(0, 0),(0, 0),(0, 0),(0, 1),(7, 200)]. The first four nodes will have order 0, the fifth and sixth elements will have orders 4 and 5, respectively. This order, in addition to the logical component, denotes the number of nodes that must be waiting and holding a lock in order for a node with this order to qualify to acquire the lock. An array of tuples does not have to be sorted at the time of the lock request, it can be updated in the background with the update of the data in the aggregator. However, if it is known that the number of nodes is small and will not reach hundreds, then the formation of such an array from the aggregator data will not affect the performance of the system as a whole.

Let's assume that we know how to get information about how many nodes are currently holding or waiting for a lock. However, during the time period for requesting this information, some nodes may have already released the lock, in which case the order will never come. Some nodes might not have captured the lock yet, in which case you need to ask again. And with such problems, this auxiliary prioritization mechanism leads to degradation of system performance.

In order for the algorithm to work deterministically and not cause problems, revision is passed to the input of the lock wait operation. The revision value is single and global for all storage nodes, and any operation on the storage returns it. It is not difficult for the worker process to get this value. And by analogy with the methods of updating values, omitting the request for the current state of the locks, a duplex connection is immediately created with a request message to subscribe events on the lock. This duplex channel receives lock status messages starting from revision. When generating a message, algorithm can use an additional parameter to specify that the storage sends messages about lock captures without sending events about their release. Thus, by the number of incoming events, algorithm can understand how many nodes have captured the lock or are waiting for the lock. The formed channel is broken at the moment when the number of messages is greater than or equal to the order of the node, and a transition is made to seizing the lock by the node itself.

All this is necessary only if the order is greater than 0. If the node understands that it is the first, then it does not need to form this channel and receive events. There will be no events. As soon as the node has received its current iteration order and determined that it is the first, then it immediately proceeds to acquire the lock.

However, in case of failures, the nodes may not have the most up-to-date information about priorities. In this case, there must be a watchdog timer, which was described earlier.

Class Diagram. Fig. 3.

Class Diagram.

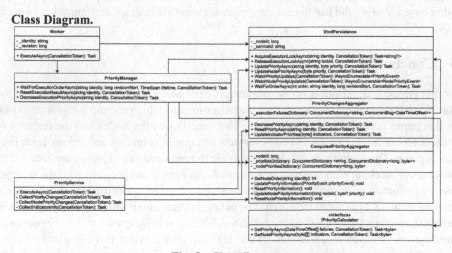

Fig. 3. Class diagram.

4   Discussion

Let's discuss the destabilizing factors and unexpected failures that the described algorithm must cope with

In the case when a node loses connection with the storage or is completely disconnected, then after the TTL for its lease expires, all data about the priority of this node will be erased from the storage. The nodes will receive messages about deleting the keys from the store and will have to delete the corresponding data from the aggregators.

In the case when the data on the nodes diverge for some reason, watchdog timers will prevent a dead lock on the system itself.

The storage is responsible for the consistency of the data, and it also ensures the prevention of most of the destabilizing factors. If a storage node fails, the system will automatically switch sending requests to another storage node. Each storage node knows about all other storage nodes, which prevents brain splits at firewalls. Each node in the system knows about each node of the storage, which ensures automatic switching of traffic to a stable functioning node. The storage has synchronous replication and each node is able to accept requests from the system. There are various discovery protocols for the service, sometimes they are specific to a particular key-value store, but usually this is either an explicit configuration or a DNS query. The service node can balance its requests between storage replicas, choosing the storage with the lowest ping.

All of the above only works well if all nodes have an identical configuration file. Keep in mind that if the nodes are configured differently, have different schedules, then the requirement for a certain iteration period will be violated. However, the requirement to perform one iteration at one particular point in time is not violated. For most data processing systems, timing violations are acceptable for the application launch period. In other cases, you should use the configuration server (externalized configuration pattern) [13].

5   Conclusion

In this paper, a description of the worker process was given. The restrictions for the functioning of worker processes is set, the situations to which the mechanism proposed in this paper is applicable are described. The specifics of the nodes and the features of their behavior are indicated. A brief overview of current solutions and the methods they use is given. The main repositories that provide the required functionality are listed. The specifics of working with storages are indicated, the operations performed on the storage, the data structure is described. The main methods of setting priorities are indicated, the method with the byte range is chosen. The general points and problems that the proposed prioritization mechanism solves are described. The basic principle on which the proposed mechanism is based is described. There are requirements for the complexity of the order determination operation. An algorithm for determining the order and calculating priorities is described. The process of obtaining information from indicators and other nodes with subsequent aggregation is described. The problems of determining the order, taking the lock are described and a solution is proposed, with an example. The main algorithms are schematically described. Destabilizing factors and system reactions to them are described.

References

1. Rai, K., Sahana, B., Pai, A.N., Gautham, S., Dhanush, U.: Vertical scaling of virtual machines in cloud environment. In: 2021 International Conference on Recent Trends on Electronics, Information, Communication & Technology (RTEICT), pp. 458–462 (2021)
2. Dawei, Y., Hengxiang, Y., Meihui, H., Jun, M.: Research on the application of distributed key-value storage technology in computer database platform. In: 2022 IEEE 2nd International Conference on Power, Electronics and Computer Applications (ICPECA), pp. 690–694 (2022)
3. Leslie, L.: Specifying Systems (2003)
4. Brendan, B.: Designing Distributed Systems: Patterns and Paradigms for Scalable. Reliable Services (2018)
5. Tadayon, T.: Time Synchronization in Distributed Systems without a Central Clock (2019)
6. Nwe, T., Yee, T.T., Htoon, E.C., Nakamura, J.: A consistent replica selection approach for distributed key-value storage system. In: 2019 International Conference on Advanced Information Technologies (ICAIT), pp. 114–119 (2019)
7. Bolfing, A.: Distributed Systems. Oxford University Press (2020)
8. Mariusz, Ś, Beata, P.: Performance comparison of programming interfaces on the example of REST API, GraphQL and gRPC. J. Comput. Sci. Inst. **21**, 356–361 (2021)
9. Alpos, O., Cachin, C., Zanolini, L.: How to trust strangers: composition of byzantine quorum systems. In: 40th International Symposium on Reliable Distributed Systems (SRDS) SRDS Reliable Distributed Systems (SRDS) (2021)
10. Sukhendu, K., Nabendu, C., Samiran, C.: Concurrency Control in Distributed System Using Mutual Exclusion. Springer, Singapore (2018)
11. Quartz.NET: https://www.quartz-scheduler.net/documentation/quartz-3.x/quick-start.html. Accessed 20 Mar 2022
12. Hangfire: https://www.hangfire.io/. Accessed 20 Mar 2022
13. Pattern: Externalized configuration. https://microservices.io/patterns/externalized-configuration.html. Accessed 20 Mar 2022
14. Etcd versus other key-value stores. https://etcd.io/docs/v3.3/learning/why. Accessed 11 Apr 2022

Analysis of Methods for Classifying
and Segmenting 3D Images

Valeriy Atroshchenko[1], Roman Dyachenko[1], Dmitry Gura[1,2(✉)], Leonid Vidovskiy[1],
Vladislav Dovgal[1], and Jean Doumit[3]

[1] Kuban State Technological University, 2, Moskovskaya Street, 350072 Krasnodar,
Russian Federation
gurada@kubstu.ru
[2] Kuban State Agrarian University, 13, Kalinina Street, 350044 Krasnodar, Russian Federation
[3] Faculty of Letters and Human Sciences Branch 2, Geospatial Lab, Lebanese University, Fanar,
Lebanon

Abstract. Issues related to the classification and segmentation of three-
dimensional images in the modern era of the transition of technological and economic systems to the digital space are a very relevant and attractive vector of
research from a scientific point of view. This article presents the main methods of
semantic classification and segmentation of three-dimensional images, describes
their main features and analyzes the effectiveness of their work on several data
sets.

Keywords: AI · Image segmentation · Semantic segmentation · 3D images ·
SDGs

1 Introduction

The representation of the space around us in the form of three-dimensional images and
the creation of new methods for segmenting and classifying such images is one of the
leading directions in which scientific and technological progress is moving. The practical
necessity of the sphere of use of the final product of 3D modeling technology, covering
many areas of human activity, causes the popularization of this area of scientific research.
Scientific research based on three-dimensional modeling can be conditionally divided
into two large groups:

- Research aimed at creating methods for obtaining three-dimensional images;
- Research in the field of processing and analysis of three-dimensional images, presented as a set of three-dimensional data (dataset), aimed at studying the methods of
  processing, segmentation and classification of three-dimensional images. The second
  group of studies is of great interest and is part of such a wide field of data science as
  Data Science.

© The Author(s), under exclusive license to Springer Nature Switzerland AG 2022
A. Gibadullin (Ed.): ITIDMS 2021, CCIS 1703, pp. 104–116, 2022.
https://doi.org/10.1007/978-3-031-21340-3_10

During the processing of a point cloud, the solution of the problems of classifying objects of a point cloud, which belongs to semantic classification, is of no small importance. Since the task of segmenting objects is extremely non-trivial, the most promising method for solving it is the use of deep neural networks, which are able to extract informative features from three-dimensional data automatically.

At the moment, there are many solutions in the field of application of machine learning algorithms for working with three-dimensional objects, which are divided into two main groups [13]:

- Indirect methods of working with a point cloud, implying the transfer of a point cloud to a different form of data representation;
- Direct methods for working with a point cloud, which take the point cloud directly as input for a neural network.

As theoretical and practical experience shows, for each task there is one or more solutions that allow you to most effectively obtain a high-quality result. The task of the analysis is to identify the best machine learning methods for classifying and segmenting a point cloud.

2   Materials and Methods

To begin with, a review of machine learning models based on direct methods for working with a point cloud was made. They can be divided into several groups depending on how the neural network architecture handles unstructured data.

2.1   Methods for Merging Graph Convolutional Neural Networks

Algorithms based on this method use spatial filters and express the representation of data on a geometric surface, revealing patterns in the surface distribution of points. The following are data on the input and output data, as well as the features of some algorithms related to this method.

DGCNN [1]. It takes a point cloud as input, the output result is a segmented point cloud and an estimated distribution of objects by class.

Has the following features:

- Has a graph that is dynamically rebuilt as data passes through the layers of the network;
- A special network converts the point cloud at the input to the canonical form;
- Hidden layers use edge convolutions to find nearest neighbors for each point in hidden feature space and Euclidean space (Fig. 1).

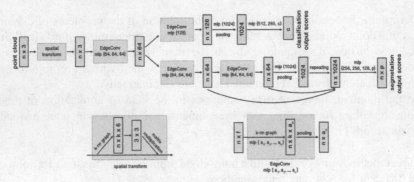

Fig. 1. DGCNN architecture.

Gapnet. It takes a point cloud as input, the output result is a segmented point cloud and an estimated distribution of objects by class.

Has the following features:

– Using the attention mechanism, which consists of two parts: self-attention for the current point and the neighbors of this point;
– A multi-head mechanism that allows obtaining both a stabilized network and structural information by combining several independent GAPLayers.

RGCNN [2]. It takes a point cloud as input, the output result is a segmented point cloud and an estimated distribution of objects by class.

Has the following features:

– The use of the Laplace matrix for a given graph for optimal recognition of the structure of the graph, dynamically changing with the passage of each layer of the graph;
– The network is built from blocks, each of which contains a graph construction operator, a convolution operator on a graph, and a feature selection operator;
– The model implements resistance to noise in the data.

2.2 Feature Fusion Methods

Algorithms based on this method are used in the analysis of large scenes. To optimize the extraction of informative features of both the general scene and individual objects, the synthesis of several models is used, each of which reveals a certain category of features. Below are data on the input and output data, as well as the features of some algorithms related to this method.

SpiderCNN [3]. It takes a point cloud as input, the output is a segmented point cloud and an estimated distribution of objects by class (Fig. 2, Fig. 3).

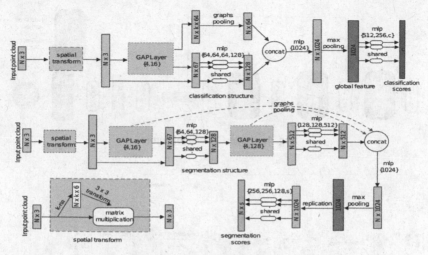

Fig. 2. GAPNet architecture.

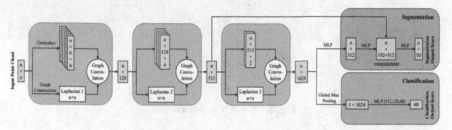

Fig. 3. Архитектура RGCNN.

Has the following features:

– The product of a piecewise constant function and a polynomial obtained as a result of the expansion of the Taylor series is used;
– Based on the work of functions described above, the SpiderConv operator was created and applied.

A-CNN [4]. It takes a point cloud as input, the output result is a segmented point cloud and an estimated distribution of objects by class.

Has the following features:

– It is necessary to carry out a preliminary calculation of the normals for the point cloud, since they are used in the calculation process;
– Use of ring convolutions (Fig. 4, Fig. 5).

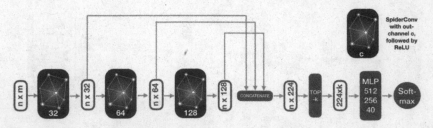

Fig. 4. SpiderCNN architecture.

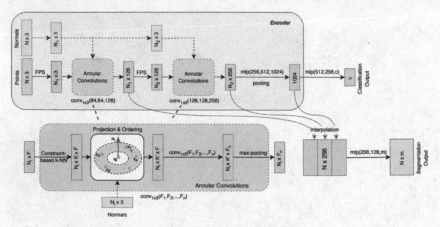

Fig. 5. A-CNN architecture.

PointSIFT. It takes a point cloud as input, the output result is a segmented point cloud and an estimated distribution of objects by class.

Has the following features:

- Can be used on scenes with a large number of objects;
- Is a modification of the PointNet model with preliminary extraction of three-dimensional SIFT features (Fig. 6).

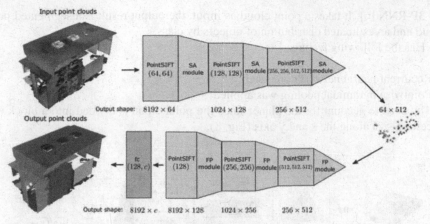

Fig. 6. PointSIFT architecture.

2.3 Methods Based on Multi-scale

The algorithms of this group are adapted for extracting informative features at different scales in the data. Below are data on the input and output data, as well as the features of some algorithms related to this method.

PointNet++ [5]. It takes a point cloud as input, the output is a segmented point cloud and an estimated distribution of objects by class.

Has the following features:

- Uses the farthest point sampling algorithm for initial splitting;
- When working with a special structure of the metric space, in some cases it helps to get a more optimal result compared to the Euclidean space (Fig. 7).

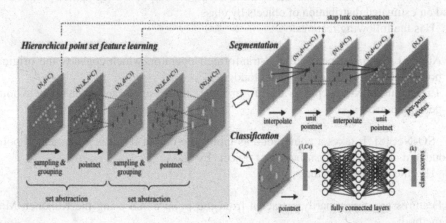

Fig. 7. PointNet++ architecture.

3P-RNN [6]. It takes a point cloud as input, the output result is a segmented point cloud and an estimated distribution of objects by class.

Has the following·features:

– Recurrent neural networks are used;
– Pointwise pyramidal pooling was applied;
– The need to account for the plane, since the point cloud is divided into a block of a certain size along the x and y axis (Fig. 8).

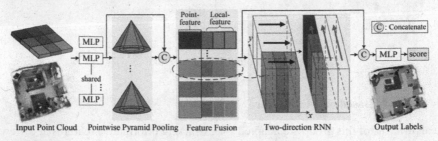

Fig. 8. 3D-RNN architecture.

2.4 Point Ordering Methods

This group is primarily aimed at solving problems with the disorder of three-dimensional data according to certain criteria that are set in each architecture to optimize the result. The following are data on the input and output data, as well as the features of some algorithms related to this method.

PointCNN [7]. It takes a point cloud as input, the output is a segmented point cloud and an estimated distribution of objects by class.

Has the following features:

– Applied multilayer perceptron X-tranformed operator, which converts the original point cloud into a weighted point cloud;
– The outputs of X-perceptrons are informative features, since they are invariant to point permutations.

SO-Net [8]. It takes a point cloud as input, the output result is a segmented point cloud and an estimated distribution of objects by class.

Has the following features:

– Features are preliminarily extracted from the point cloud using the Kohonen Map method;
– Applicable to a wide range of tasks: clustering, classification, form completion (Fig. 9, Fig. 10).

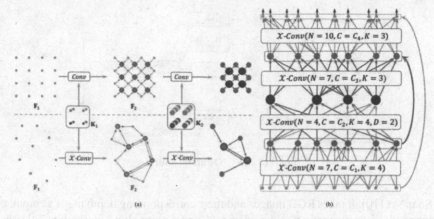

Fig. 9. PointCNN architecture.

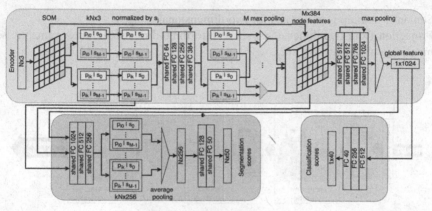

Fig. 10. SO-Net architecture.

Compared to the variety of solutions based on direct methods, there are significantly fewer algorithms developed using indirect methods. They can be divided into two groups: multi-view based methods, and volumetric methods.

2.5 Multi-view Based Methods

This method is based on obtaining a set of two-dimensional slices of the original point cloud from different angles. This approach allows using image processing algorithms.

MVCNN [9]. It takes RGB images and their corresponding depth maps as input, the output is a semantic markup of images and a point cloud marked into classes.

Has the following features:

- Works optimally when classifying and clustering single related models;
- The results of working with polygonal models are better than the results of working with a point cloud (Fig. 11).

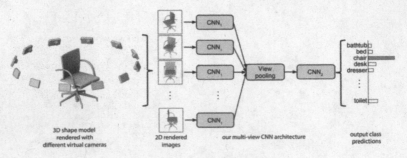

Fig. 11. MVCNN architecture.

SnapNet [10]. It takes RGB images and their corresponding depth maps as input, the output result is the semantic markup of images and a point cloud marked into classes.

Has the following features:

- Semantic markup is performed for two-dimensional images;
- Projection from two-dimensional space into three-dimensional after semantic segmentation of images (Fig. 12).

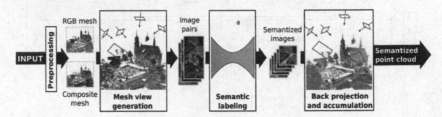

Fig. 12. SnapNet architecture.

2.6 Volumetric Methods

This group of indirect methods uses voxel representation of 3D models. The approach simplifies convolution generalization and processing.

SEGCloud [11]. It takes a voxelized model as input, the output result is the voxel mask of the recognized object and the estimated distribution of objects by class.

Has the following features:

- The application of optimal separation to the voxel network is carried out by the 3D-FCNN architecture;
- Trilinear interpolator is used (Fig. 13).

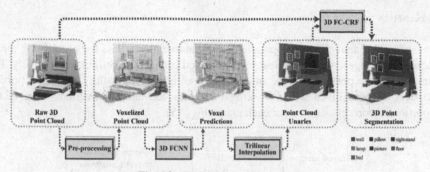

Fig. 13. SEGCloud architecture.

Point Grid [12]. It takes a voxelized model as input, the output result is the voxel mask of the recognized object and the estimated distribution of objects by class.

Has the following features:

– The procedure of sampling points in space was applied;
– The addition of the original point cloud is used (Fig. 14).

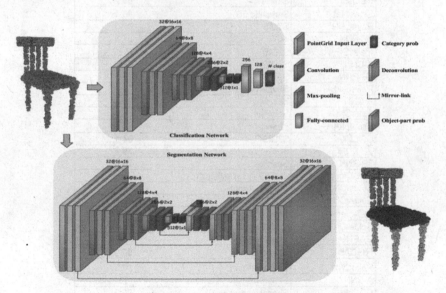

Fig. 14. PointGrid architecture.

3 Results

In the course of analyzing the operation of the above algorithms for classifying three-dimensional images, several data sets were applied for each algorithm, respectively. The definitions of the performance of an artificial intelligence algorithm are the proportion of correct answers given while working with data sets and the average value of the proportion of correct answers for each class (Fig. 15).

Method name	Dataset	Percentage of correct answers
SO-Net	ModelNet10	95.8
A-CNN	ModelNet10	95.5
PointNet++	SHREC15	94.49
PointCNN	ModelNet40 (pre-aligned)	93.5
A-CNN	ModelNet40	92.6
PointGrid	ModelNet40	92.5
SO-Net	ModelNet40	92.4
GAPNet	ModelNet40	92.4
PointCNN	ModelNet40 (unaligned)	92.2
RGCNN	ModelNet40	91.2
MVCNN	ModelNet40	90.1
PointSIFT	ScanNet	89.2
SnapNet	Semantic 3D	88.1
PointCNN	S3DIS	88.1
3P-RNN	vKITTI XYZ-RGB	87.8
PointSIFT	S3DIS	87.72
A-CNN	S3DIS	87.3
3P-RNN	S3DIS	86.9
PointGrid	ShapeNet-55	86.0
A-CNN	ScanNet	85.4
PointCNN	ScanNet	85.1
PointNet++	ScanNet	84.5
DGCNN	S3DIS	84.1
3P-RNN	vKITTI XYZ-only	79.6
3P-RNN	ScanNet	76.5
SEGCloud	NYUV2 (13 классов)	66.82
SpiderCNN	ShapeNet-part	96.4
SpiderCNN	SHREC15	95.8
SO-Net	ShapeNet-part	94.3
SpiderCNN	ModelNet40	92.4
GAPNet	ShapeNet-part	92.1
RGCNN	ShapeNet-part	90.9
PointCNN	ShapeNet-part	90.6
A-CNN	ShapeNet-part	86
DGCNN	ShapeNet-part	85.2
SEGCloud	KITTI	67.32
SEGCloud	S3DIS	66.12

Fig. 15. Test results on datasets.

4 Discussion

During the analysis, it was found that solutions based on the point ordering method and the feature fusion method on the presented data sets showed a higher result compared to other methods. However, it is worth considering the shortcomings of some solutions related to the point ordering method: suboptimal quality of work with fine details and model complexity. In solutions based on the feature fusion method, the processing of small parts is more efficient, and the processing time is also faster [13, 14]. According to the authors, solutions based on volumetric methods are not optimal for solving classification and segmentation problems in datasets similar to those given in the tests.

5 Conclusion

Summing up, it should be noted that data on the quality of work of artificial intelligence algorithms may differ when using other data sets and when solving problems other than those considered in this article. This means that it is worth considering the general trend in the effectiveness of the presented methods in solving problems of processing three-dimensional images. In the presented datasets, the methods of ordering points and the methods of feature fusion turned out to be the most optimal methods for working with three-dimensional data.

Acknowledgement. The research was carried out using the equipment of the Research Center for Food and Chemical Technologies of KubSTU (CKP_3111) which development is supported by the Ministry of Science and Higher Education of the Russian Federation (Agreement No. 075–15-2021–679).

The research was carried out at the expense of the grant of the Russian Science Foundation No. 22–29-00849 "Development of an intelligent information system for decision-making support for solving complex problems of territorial planning using strong artificial intelligence" .

References

1. Author, F.: Article title. Journal **2**(5), 99–110 (2016)
2. Author, F., Author, S.: Title of a proceedings paper. In: Editor, F., Editor, S. (eds.) CONFERENCE 2016, LNCS, vol. 9999, pp. 1–13. Springer, Heidelberg (2016)
3. Author, F., Author, S., Author, T.: Book title, 2nd edn. Publisher, Location (1999)
4. Author, F.: Contribution title. In: 9th International Proceedings on Proceedings, pp. 1–2. Publisher, Location (2010)
5. LNCS Homepage: http://www.springer.com/lncs. Last accessed 21 Nov 2016
6. The Urban Planning Code of the Russian Federation dated 29.12.2004 N 190-FZ. http://www.consultant.ru/document/cons_doc_LAW_51040. Last accessed 6 Dec 2021
7. Pogrebnaya, N.: Purpose of territorial planning and types of documents of territorial planning. In: Scientific Results of 2017, pp. 120–124 (2017)
8. Karmanov, A., Knyshev, A., Eliseeva, V.: Geographic Information Systems of Territorial Administration. ITMO University, St. Petersburg (2015)
9. Prokopenko, N.: Decision Support Systems. In: Novgorod, N. (ed.) NNGASU (2017)

10. Tikhanychev, O.: Theory and Practice of Automating Decision Support. Editus, Moscow (2018)
11. Ershov, D., Kachalov, R.: Decision Support Systems within the Procedures of Complex Strategy Building. CEMI Russian Academy of Science, Moscow (2013)
12. Popkov, A.: The use of neural networks and artificial intelligence for the purposes of territorial planning. Uchenye zapiski, Electronic scientific journal of Kursk State University 28, 48–55 (2013)
13. Burstein, F., Holsapple, C.W.: Handbook on Decision Support Systems. Springer Verlag, Berlin (2008)
14. Bolotova, L.: Decision Support Systems, vol. 1, 2. Yurayt Publishing House, Moscow (2019)
15. Solodunov, A., Prshitadok, S., Sarksyan, L., Lukyanova, M.: Application of laser scanning for monitoring engineering structures. Colloquium J. 50, 78–80 (2019)
16. Gribkova, L., Gorstka, N.: Disadvantages, advantages and possibilities of laser scanning. In: Scientific Discussion of Modern Youth: Actual Issues, Achievements and Innovations, pp. 48–50 (2018)
17. Wang, C., Wen, C., Dai, Y., Yu, S., Liu, M.: Urban 3D modeling with mobile laser scanning: a review. Virtual Reality Intell. Hardw. 3, 175–212 (2020)
18. Rudenko, Y., Bogdanets, E.: The relevance of lidar imaging at this stage of laser scanning development. Tech. Sci. Theory Pract. 53, 20–29 (2016)
19. Gura, D., Markovskiy, I., Pshidatok, S.: Methods of monitoring real estate objects using three-dimensional laser scanning in the specifics of urban lands. Geod. Cartogr. 82, 45–53 (2021)
20. Pogorelov, A., Kiselev, E., Lipilin, D., Boiko, E.: 3D city modeling. Greening assessment. Institutions of local democracy in managing the environmentally sustainable development of local territories. In: Materials of the II All-Russian Scientific and Practical Conference with International Participation, Krasnodar, pp. 198–203 (2021)
21. Jaiwei, H., Micheline, K., Jian, P.: Data Mining: Concepts and Techniques (3rd edn.). Morgan Kaufmann (2011)
22. Kim, H., Kim, C.: 3D as-built modeling from incomplete point clouds using connectivity relations. Autom. Constr. 130 (2021)
23. Miltseva, L.A.: Information system for decision support based on a multi-agent approach. East. European J. Adv. Technol. 41, 22–26 (2009)
24. Assumma, V., Bottero, M., Angelis, E.De, Lourenço, J.M., Monaco, R., Soares, A.J.: A decision support system for territorial resilience assessment and planning: an application to the Douro Valley (Portugal). Sci. Total Environ. 756, 143806 (2021)
25. Sivkov, A.: Possibilities of machine learning methods for forecasting the development of urban areas. Interexpo Geo-Siberia 2, 77–81 (2020)
26. Diasio, S.R., Agell, N.: The evolution of expertise in decision support technologies: a challenge for organizations. In: 13th International Conference on Computer Supported Cooperative Work in Design, 4968139 (2009)
27. Gura, D., Dubenko, Y., Markovskiy, I., Pshidatok, S.: Monitoring infrastructure facilities of territories in agricultural sector. IOP Conf. Ser. Earth Environ. Sci. 403, 012185 (2019)

Tone Image Processing with Discrete Data Structure

Tatiana A. Shornikova(✉) 📧 and Yuliya S. Gusynina 📧

Penza State Technological University, 1a/11, Baidukova Pas./Gagarina Street, 440039 Penza, Russian Federation
shornikovat@mail.ru

Abstract. The article focuses on the problem of image processing using a discrete data structure for tone images. The problem of conversion of continuous image into discrete form is considered. Two procedures are described: selecting a discrete grid for representing an image, and quantization, which consists in displaying luminance and color values in integers. The solution to the problem of selecting the visual display resolution and the number of levels of gray tone or colors when processing one-dimensional data is presented. A review of the transformation methods was carried out, after which the sample for both the one-dimensional case and the two-dimensional one was considered. The basis of the transformation methods was the Fourier and Hadamard transformations. These transformations are used in the design of filters designed to improve the quality of images, as well as in the implementation of data compression methods. They form the basis of image recovery from projections.

Keywords: Image processing · Discrete grid · Quantization · Image sampling · Fourier transform · Fourier image · Signal spectrum · Shannon theorem

1 Introduction

The use of transformations and linear filtering procedures is discussed in detail in most books on image processing. So, M. Pratt well consecrated the problems to which this article is devoted. He discussed the perception of images subjected to "rough" sampling. The early works of K. Knowlton and L. Harmon also provide an interesting overview of these issues. They cover some aspects of image alignment using low frequency pseudo-random noise overlay. In their literature on machine graphics, much attention is paid to the theory of the selective method for proper reproduction of images.

If an image is to be processed using digital technologies, it is often represented by a matrix or other discrete data structure. However, the image primarily has some signal transmitting information to a certain observer, and in many applied problems this condition is extremely significant.

A. Gibadullin (Ed.): ITIDMS 2021, CCIS 1703, pp. 117–127, 2022.
https://doi.org/10.1007/978-3-031-21340-3_11

2 Materials and Methods

Consider a problem that consists of converting a continuous image into a discrete form and involves two procedures: sampling, which is reduced to selecting a discrete grid to represent the image, and quantization, which consists in displaying luminance and color values in integers. Similar tasks involve selecting the visual resolution and the number of grayscale levels and colors. These procedures are also used in the processing of univariate data and, accordingly, are carefully studied in this case, but when working with two-dimensional data, new tasks arise [1].

If $f(t)$ – is a function defined on the interval $[0, \infty)$, then its fourier image has the form

$$F(w) = \int_{t=0}^{\infty} f(t)e^{-wt}dt, \quad 0 \le w < \infty \tag{1}$$

If $f(x, y)$ – is a function of two variables defined on an infinite plane, then its image in a two-dimensional transformation has the form.

$$F(u, v) = \int_{-\infty}^{\infty} \int_{-\infty}^{\infty} f(x, y)\, e^{-t(xu+yv)}dxdy, \, 0 \le u, v < \infty \tag{2}$$

The term spectrum is often used as a synonym for the concept of Fourier transform. Then the transformation for the one-dimensional case has the form

$$F(u) = \sum_{k=0}^{N-1} f(k)\, \exp(-i\frac{2\pi}{N}uk), \, 0 \le u \le N-1 \tag{3}$$

and for the two-dimensional case

$$F(u, v) = \sum_{k=0}^{N-1}\sum_{l=0}^{N-1} f(k, l)\, \exp(i\frac{2\pi}{N}(ku + lv)), \quad 0 \le u, \, v \le N-1. \tag{4}$$

The last two equations are usually called the discrete Fourier transform. The summation limits of each of the two sums can be different, which allows you to define this transformation on a rectangular area. You cannot, however, define a two-dimensional Fourier transform on a freeform region. If you limit the integration limits in (2) or the summation limits in (4), then the result of the transformation will depend not only on the values of the function f, , but also on the shape of the summation area (integration) [2].

The discrete inverse Fourier transform is defined as follows:

$$f(k) = \frac{1}{N} \sum_{u=0}^{N-1} F(u)\, \exp(i\frac{2\pi}{N}uk), \quad 0 \le k \le N-1, \tag{5}$$

$$f(k, l) = \frac{1}{N^2} \sum_{u=0}^{N-1}\sum_{v=0}^{N-1} F(u, v)\, \exp(i\frac{2\pi}{N}(uk + vl)), \quad 0 \le k, \, l \le N-1, \tag{6}$$

The equations defining the transformation can be written in many ways, some of which help to introduce transformations of other kinds, as well as determine computationally effective methods for implementing them. Denote the indicative function $\exp(-i\frac{2\pi}{N})$ through z and define the matrix Z:

$$
Z = \begin{pmatrix}
1 & 1 & 1 & \cdots & 1 \\
1 & z & z^2 & \cdots & z^{N-1} \\
1 & z^2 & z^4 & \cdots & z^{2N-1} \\
\cdots & \cdots & \cdots & \cdots & \cdots \\
1 & z^{N-1} & z^{2N-1} & \cdots z^{(N-1)(N-1)}
\end{pmatrix}. \tag{7}
$$

In other words, $Z_{uk} = z^{uh}$. In most applications N it is not only an even number, but also equal to the step of the number 2. The matrix Z can be simplified by considering that $2^N = 1$, $z^{\frac{N}{2}} = -1$, $z^{\frac{N}{4}} = -i$ and $z^{\frac{3N}{4}} = i$. Note also that this matrix is symmetric, and the scalar product of any of its columns (or rows) and some other column (or row) is zero. The scalar product of any of its columns (or rows) with itself is N. Thus, the matrix Z has the important property that its inverse matrix is equal to its conjugate transposed matrix multiplied by $\frac{1}{N}$. A matrix of the form $\frac{1}{sqrt(N)}Z$, in which the inverse matrix is equal to its conjugate transposed matrix is unitary. Denote through f a column vector whose components are values $F(u)$. Now Eq. (3) can be written in matrix form

$$
\mathbf{F} = \mathbf{Zf}. \tag{8}
$$

In the two-dimensional case, the Fourier transform is equivalent to multiplying all columns of a function $f(k, l)$ by a matrix Z, followed by multiplying on the right all rows of the function by Z' (the result of the transposition of the matrix Z) [3]. As a result, Eq. (4) takes the form

$$
\mathbf{F} = \mathbf{ZfZ'}. \tag{9}
$$

The expressions for f and F represent the image matrix and the matrix resulting from the transformation, respectively. Similar expressions can be obtained for an inverse transformation if you replace the matrix Z with its complex conjugate transposed matrix Z^*, taken several times.

A special case of such a transformation is the Hadamard transform. The matrices for this transformation can be recursively set as follows:

$$
Z_2 = \begin{pmatrix} 1 & -1 \\ 1 & -1 \end{pmatrix}, \tag{10'}
$$

$$
Z_{2N} = \begin{pmatrix} Z_N & Z_N \\ Z_N & -Z_N \end{pmatrix}. \tag{10''}
$$

Thus, the Hadamard transform corresponds to the decomposition by periodic functions of a rectangular shape, in contrast to the Fourier transform, which provides for decomposition by sinusoidal and cosine components. Moreover, the matrix Z can be set in a form similar to expression (7) by placing $Z = -1$ and taking another rule for changing the measures of degree. The main advantage of the Hadamard transform is the replacement of multiplications of complex quantities with changes in signs. In all other respects, this transformation allows you to obtain exactly the same results as the Fourier transform.

These transformations are mainly used in the design of filters designed to improve the quality of images, as well as in the implementation of some methods of data compression. They also form the basis of image recovery from projections. Using transformations to compress data is justified when most components $F(u)$ are zero. When this condition is met, you can use Eq. (5) or (6) to restore values $f(k)$ to less than N – the number of values of the fourier image. However, more information may be needed to describe each element of the fourier image than is necessary to provide the values of the original function. As a result, the compression ratio may not be as large as expected.

Using the defining equations to implement the transformation given by Eq. (8) requires N^2 computational operations in the one-dimensional case and N^4 – in the two-dimensional case. A more efficient algorithm - the fast Fourier transform - can be obtained by rearranging the terms of the sum in Eq. (3) and using the fact that the product uk takes the same values at different values u and k. This transformation requires only $N \log_2 N$ operations. The fast Fourier transform algorithm can be used to obtain a two-dimensional fourier image: first, the image of each row of the image is determined, and then – for all columns. This method is illustrated by an algorithm in which the fast Fourier transform procedure (N, x) replaces the N – elementary matrix x with its discrete fourier image.

Each reference to a fast Fourier transform procedure Фурье (N, x) requires computational effort costs proportional to $N \log_2 N$. Since the total number of such calls is $2N$, computational complexity is generally in the order $N^2 \log_2(N^2)$.

When working with the sampling of values in the process of further processing, we use only the signal values fixed in the selected points [4].

3   Results

3.1   Sampling in One Dimensional Case

The fundamental mathematical result for the one-dimensional case is Shannon's reference theorem, formulated in terms of the signal spectrum. Let be $d(t)$ – a discrete representation $f(t)$, formed by unquantized pulses separated by intervals of length T one, i.e.

$$d(kT) = f(kT), \quad k = 0, 1, \ldots, \infty; \tag{11'}$$

$$d(t) = 0, \quad \text{if } t \neq kT. \tag{11''}$$

In this case, it can be shown that $D(w)$ – the fourier image $d(t)$ is associated with $F(w)$ the following relation:

$$D(w) = \sum_{n=-\infty}^{\infty} F(w - \frac{2\pi n}{T}). \tag{12}$$

In other words, the fourier image of the discrete transformation $d(t)$ is obtained by summing the fourier images $f(t)$, taken with a shift. The relation (12) is not related to the discrete fourier image $d(t)$; it characterizes the continuous transformation of some function that takes non-zero values only at certain discrete points in time. The difference in the results of the transformation of functions d and f can be understood by referring to the examples given in Fig. 1. On the first graph $F_1(w) = 0$ at $w > \frac{P_i}{T}$, while on the second graph it is not. Graphs for these two cases are given below. In the first case, if $D(w)$ specified, then $F(w)$ you can define accurately and, therefore, restore $d(t)$. This is not possible in the second case due to overlapping of the terms of Eq. (12).

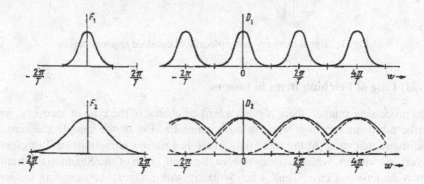

Fig. 1. Fourier transform of sampled signals

It turns out that the signal can be restored if the time between neighboring samples is less than $\frac{P_i}{w_{\max}}$, i.e. the sampling frequency is at least twice the value $w_{\max}$.

Suppose that the recovered signal consists of constant values equal to the sample values (see Fig. 2). Let $f(t) = E \sin(wt)$ with a certain value w. If it is necessary that the maximum deviation of the recovered signal from the original signal does not exceed the predetermined value ε, then, as follows from Fig. 2, the following relation must be performed:

$$|f(kT \pm \frac{T}{2}) - f(kT)| < \varepsilon, \tag{13}$$

where k – moment, and T – sampling interval [5].

Then, using the mean theorem, it turns out that this inequality is fulfilled if the maximum of an absolute value $f(t)$ - is arbitrary $f'(t)$, less than $\frac{2\varepsilon}{T}$. For our signal $f(t)$ you can also use the trigonometric formula to calculate the maximum value of the difference in inequality (13) and show that it is equivalent to inequality $E |\sin(w\frac{T}{2})| < \varepsilon$.

If the sine value of a small angle is approximated by the value of the actual angle, then the last inequality takes the form

$$T < \frac{2\varepsilon}{Ew}, \tag{14}$$

and the boundary defined by this inequality is substantially smaller than Shannon's. The use of the mean theorem leads to this result.

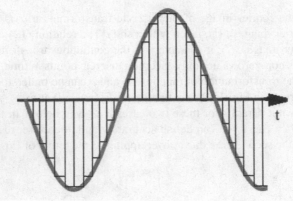

Fig. 2. Signal recovery using piecemeal constant approximation

3.2 2D Case of Fetching Items in Images

When processing images, there is often a limited choice of the type of recovery, which must be taken into account when using a generalization of the sample theorem to a two-dimensional case. At the same time, there is a narrow-directional use of classical recovery algorithms, which reduces to zero the application of the Shannon theorem for the two-dimensional case. Thus, when working with images, the sampling frequency should usually be significantly higher than that determined by the results of spectral analysis. In particular, it is possible to sample at a frequency corresponding to the upper boundary, which is determined by the ratio of the form (14).

The sample interval obtained in this way will be equal to the value determined by the sample theorem and multiplied by a factor $\frac{2\varepsilon}{\pi E}$. If the ratio $\frac{\varepsilon}{E}$ is 0.01, then the sampling should be carried out at a frequency exceeding the limit value of the sampling frequency determined by Shannon's theorem by 157 times [6].

The explanation for the poor quality of the pictures is not a small sample of elements, as it may seem at first glance, but a piecemeal-constant restoration. A simple confirmation of this assumption can be the following: if you squint your eyes or move a short distance, then the picture takes on a more obvious shape. After all, it will contain a large share of information.

Thus, it is possible to obtain algorithms that perform linear interpolation between the values of the sample elements, and as a result, when reproducing a low-definition image on a high-resolution screen, additional pixels are assigned intermediate values relative to the sample elements.

However, the interpolation process can proceed quite slowly and therefore its use when working with a standard display is impractical. Only with the help of graphic displays that perform such interpolation locally with the help of an embedded element, images with a frequency closer to the value determined by the Shannon theorem can be sampled. Using digital filtering terms, such devices are equivalent to higher order synchronization elements.

But the oversampling, which is often referred to, prevents the creation of a purely digital system for processing pictorial information. The solution can be found in mixing the analog and digital output signals with the help of special equipment. In this case, the signals will come to the device from two sources: the controller of the raster graphics device and the television transmitting camera or tape for analog video recording. These signals can be mixed by superimposing, for example, statistical information, which is obtained by discrete means, on the analog one [7].

The assignment of sample points will not cause difficulties in the case of one-dimensional signals, and for the case of two-dimensional signals, some difficulties will arise. Therefore, for further reasoning, we introduce some notation.

Take a plane K containing an analog image. Then the discretization element will be a compact convex subset K, which is used to calculate the value of the sample element included in the image with selected elements. Accordingly, the union of such elements will be a selective grid. Then any selective element is an image element (pixel). Next, consider the visual display plane D, where pixels are mapped to image reproduction elements and the result is an analog image being restored.

In this case, there is an intersection of discretization elements. Indeed, in most sampling devices, they can partially overlap, with the exception of the elements of the image reproduction, which most often do not overlap. Figure 3 shows an example of a typical sampling grid and a display corresponding to it. Here it can be noted that there are sharp edges in the display, which correspond to the high frequencies introduced by the sample. The given grids for sampling and display are not always different, and most often their differentiation leads to distortion of the picture [8].

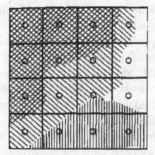 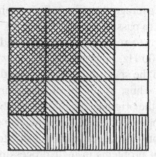

Fig. 3. Selection grid display

The point transfer function $f(l)$ is used to describe most of the sampling steps and displays the measure of the contribution of different points to the value of the sample point, depending on their distance l from it. This function is decreasing and equals zero outside the sampling element. If the decay rate of the function $f(l)$ is large, then the overlap of the sampling elements is excluded. In this case, in the general case, the term "element" means both a sampling element and an image reproduction element.

In image processing, a square grid is most often used, consisting of elements - squares, ordered in the form of a checkerboard. It is also possible to use a hexagonal grid. The indisputable advantage of this grid is the adjoining of adjacent elements in the same way. For a square grid, it is necessary to distinguish the side or angle of adjoining adjacent elements. A significant disadvantage of the hexagonal grid is the difference in the distances between the centers of the elements vertically and horizontally.

The type and size of the grid used affects the shape and type of the transfer function of the point, so in what follows we will consider only square grids [9].

4 Discussion

4.1 Image Distortion Due to Insufficient Sampling Rate

Consider the case of image distortion, when high frequencies are convolved with low ones. This occurs when the sampling interval is incorrectly chosen. In this case, the high-frequency signal, after sampling at too low a frequency, becomes a low-frequency one.

In practice, such a situation is encountered when processing images that include text. If the readings are made too infrequently, then the result looks like a chaotic combination of dark and light areas, and not the outlines of letters. Another option is to sample the image, in which the reproduction of the gray tone level is achieved by changing the density of black and white dots. If the sampling rate is commensurate with the size of the dots, then the sampled values will correspond to white or black, but their distribution will differ from the distribution of white and black dots in the original image. As a result, the quality of the sampled image may be very poor. Therefore, when processing text, an increase in the sampling rate is required. In the second case, one should turn to other methods: to average the values of the points of the processed image. In other words, it is necessary to pass the signals through a low-pass filter before sampling [10].

Let's turn to research. We only need frequencies below 1000 Hz, and the signal comes at 1800 Hz. Sampling at 2000 Hz introduces a false low-frequency component of 200 Hz in the spectrum of the sampled signal, which is generated by the component at 1800 Hz. Thus, to get rid of this spurious component, before proceeding with the sampling of the original signal, it should be passed through an analog low-pass filter that provides suppression of all frequencies exceeding 1000 Hz.

Distortions that occur in images due to an insufficiently high sampling rate give rise to significant problems in their processing associated with the construction of analog filters for signal preprocessing. Defocusing the optical system of an image sampling device is equivalent to passing the image through a simple low-pass filter – in some cases, this technique is sufficient.

The case of image distortion, when high frequencies are convolved with low ones, is sometimes associated with distortions resulting from piecewise constant restoration. That is, the change in the image is not associated with the mapping of some high-frequency component to some low-frequency component, but with the appearance of additional high-frequency components generated by the restoration method used. The interchangeability of these concepts is due to the fact that one of the methods for solving the problem under consideration is to increase the sampling rate, while a similar method is used to eliminate image distortions that occur due to an insufficiently high sampling rate. The difference between these processes becomes clear when one considers that the appearance of the images obtained from the selected elements is improved by defocusing, i.e. low-pass filtering of the digital image. Such filtering can only eliminate distortion caused by an insufficiently high sampling rate if it is applied to an analog image [9].

4.2 Quantization

Consider the process of quantization, when the values obtained in the process of sampling an analog signal must be represented using a finite number of bits, determined by the capabilities of the computing equipment used. In a simpler case, this procedure can be considered as a mapping of real numbers to the area of integers. The choice of the number of gray levels for the representation of black and white images should be carried out taking into account the characteristics of human vision [11].

If you take black and white images and quantize them at different levels, then when compared to the original you will notice that they look worse than it, mainly due to the visible edges that separate gray levels. However, the differences will be more noticeable when both images are displayed side by side on the monitor at the same time [12].

You can improve the appearance of images subjected to coarse quantization by adding low-frequency pseudo-random noise. Before quantization, low-frequency noise $d(x, y)$ is added to the function $z(x, y)$ representing the image at the point (x, y). To obtain this noise, you can use a random process or determine its appropriate value based on the position of the point (x, y). In any case, this value has nothing to do with $z(x, y)$. This process usually results in the disappearance of contours, and as a result, despite the imposition of noise on the image, its overall appearance is improved. One of the following numbers can be taken with equal probability as the value of the noise component $d(x, y)$:

$$-2^{(6-b)}, -2^{(5-b)}0, 2^{(5-b)}, 2^{(6-b)},$$

where b is the number of bits to be displayed [9].

The b most significant bits of the corresponding sum are taken as the pixel value. If the sum turns out to be negative, then it is equal to zero before applying the bit mask.

But even here options are possible: how to choose the ratio of the sampling frequency to the number of quantization levels. If only a fixed number of bits can be used to store a given image, then the question arises – how best to distribute them.

Thus, the choice is determined by the type of image, but, in addition, when working with a specific image, it is possible to use different sampling rates and the number of quantization levels for its individual parts. Another limitation is the amount of computation required. When solving most problems, the computational costs depend to a certain extent on the number of sample elements (pixels), but they do not reflect the number of bits spent to represent one pixel [13].

This is confirmed by the following. When sampling bi-level images on the example of pages with text, the nature of the scatter function of the sampling device leads to sampling elements that take values in a wide range. That is, the image of the 2nd class is fed to the input, and the image of the 1st class is accepted for work. In this case, you can try to return to the class 2 image, spending only one bit per pixel and equating it to zero if the input signal is less than some threshold and to one otherwise [14].

Obviously, the pixels corresponding to those bins that are located near the boundaries of the areas of the original image receive the values 0 and 1 in an arbitrary way. This can lead to the appearance or disappearance of gaps, respectively absent or present in the reference image. Therefore, the bins can be chosen small enough so that even in the narrowest parts of the region, the bin falls entirely within a region of the same color. On the other hand, you can enter 4 quantization levels at a lower resolution.

5 Conclusion

In the process of research, the issue of converting a continuous image into a discrete form using a sampling grid, which allows obtaining the intersection of sampling elements, is considered. In this case, the resulting image distortions due to an insufficiently high sampling rate are proposed to be explained by an erroneously chosen sampling interval.

The values that are obtained in the process of sampling an analog signal can be represented using a finite number of bits, determined by the capabilities of the computing equipment used, that is, quantization can be performed. And in the future, to improve the appearance of images, the imposition of low-frequency pseudo-random noise is applied, the parameters of which depend both on the type of image and on the number of quantization levels.

References

1. Martyshkin, A.I.: Associative coprocessor block based on PLD for different computer systems. ARPN J. Eng. Appl. Sci. **13**(18), 4941–4947 (2018)
2. Trokoz, D.A., et al.: Formalized description of cyber-physical systems models using temporary non-deterministic automata. J. of Phys.: Conf. Ser. **1889**(2), 022068 (2021)
3. Prokofiev, O.V., Savochkin A.E.: On how harmonic interference does influence the forming of pulse-width modulation signal. In: Proceedings – 2020 International Russian Automation Conference (RusAutoCon 2020) pp. 187–190 (2020). https://doi.org/10.1109/RusAutoCon49 822.2020.9208168
4. Mikheev, M.Y., Meshcheryakova, E.N.: The method of data management organization of a control system of highvoltage equipment malfunctions and power supply quality for an engineering unit. J Adv. Res. Dyn. Control Syst. **11**(5), 113–118 (2019)
5. Tensina, I., Vidiasova, L., Bershadskaya, E.: Information technologies in G2C communications: cybersocial trust survey. Commun. Comput. Inform. Sci. **1038**, 107–119 (2019)
6. Ushenina, I.V.: Multi-input multiplexers and selectors as basic shifter blocks in arithmetic devices operating in floating point: comparative analysis. J. Phys.: Conf. Ser. **1399**(3), 033055 (2019)
7. Pashchenko, D.V., Martyshkin, A.I., Trokoz, D.A.: Decomposition of process control algorithms for parallel computing systems using automata models. In: 2020 International Russian Automation Conference (RusAutoCon 2020), pp. 839–845 (2020). https://doi.org/10.1109/RusAutoCon49822.2020.9208165
8. Martyshkin, A.I.: Hardware buffer memory of the multiprocessor system. ARPN J. Eng. Appl. Sci. **13**(23), 9151–9156 (2018)
9. Mikheev, M., Gusynina, J., Shornikova, T.: Research on the development of recurring neural networks. CEUR Workshop Proc. **2922**, 32–43 (2021)
10. Roganov, V., Mikheev, M., Babich, M., Butaev, M., Esimova, N., Kukuchkina, O.: On the assessment of the image model of 3D models synthesized by optical-software-technical systems. In: Moscow Workshop on Electronic and Networking Technologies, MWENT 2020 – Proceedings (2020). https://doi.org/10.1109/MWENT47943.2020.9067481

11. Kindaev, A., Moiseev, A., Kolobova, E.: Using neural network technologies to reduce information asymmetry. CEUR Workshop Proc. **2922**, 1–6 (2021)
12. Vorontsov, A.A., Slesarev, Y.N.: Mathematical modeling and experimental check of output signals of magnetostrictive converters of movement. In: Proceedings - 2019 International Russian Automation Conference (RusAutoCon 2019) (2019). https://doi.org/10.1109/RUS AUTOCON.2019.8867715
13. Martyshkin, A.I., Salnikov, I.I., Pashchenko, D.V., Trokoz, D.A.: cAssociative co-processor on the basis of programmable logical integrated circuits for special purpose computer systems. In: Proceedings – 2018 Global Smart Industry Conference (GloSIC 2018) (2018). https://doi.org/10.1109/GloSIC.2018.8570067
14. Roganov, V., Kuvshinova, O., Esimova, N., Lavendels, J.: 3D Systems that imitate visually observable objects to train a person's ability to visually determine distance to a selected object. In: Proceedings --2019 21st International Conference "Complex Systems: Control and Modeling Problems" (CSCMP) 600–603 (2019)

The Concept of Client-Server Architecture for Remote Control of a Distributed Knowledge Base

Artem Voinov[1](✉) and Ilya Senokosov[2]

[1] Penza State University, 40 Krasnaya Street, Penza 440026, Russian Federation
voj49@yandex.ru
[2] 3 Lermontova Street, Penza 440026, Russian Federation

Abstract. The concept of a client-server architecture for storing and managing data of a distributed knowledge base is proposed. The client-server organization uses the principle of the "readers-writers" task with the priority of writers. The advantages of the proposed concept in comparison with analogues are presented. The server part consists of a read server, a write server, a verification server, a cache server. The client part consists of an IO module, a reader module, and a writer module. The paper shows an example of the implementation of a simplified concept. Smart Grid ontology was chosen as the knowledge base used. Apache Jena Fuseki is used as a tool for organizing the server part. This server supports the organization of requests through the user interface and through the Rest protocol. To organize the execution of requests via the Rest protocol to the server, the Insomnia software tool was used. Examples of read and write requests are shown. All queries for examples are made in SPARQL.

Keywords: Client-server architecture · Distributed knowledge base · Readers-writers · Smart Grid · Apache Jena Fuseki · SPARQL · RDF

1 Introduction

The use of client-server architecture is relevant due to the widespread introduction of information networks. This concept implies the presence of clients that make requests and receive responses, and servers that process these requests. It is traditionally accepted that data transfer between a client and a server on a network occurs via the TCP/IP protocol. The query language may vary depending on the purpose of the network. In this paper, the Rest protocol (REpresentational State Transfer) [1] is used as the interaction language. Rest is a simple data transfer protocol between a client and a server. TCP/IP is directly used as a transport, which can significantly reduce the amount of information transmitted, while maintaining its meaning. Another advantage of Rest is that any data format (JSON, multyform, etc.) can be passed to the body. The information stored on the server is presented as an ontology [2]. Ontology is a knowledge base built on the basis of Horn clauses. As a basis, an RDF graph is used, built on triplets "subject – predicate – object". The statement "Soil type is chernozem" in RDF terminology can be represented

© The Author(s), under exclusive license to Springer Nature Switzerland AG 2022
A. Gibadullin (Ed.): ITIDMS 2021, CCIS 1703, pp. 128–137, 2022.
https://doi.org/10.1007/978-3-031-21340-3_12

as follows: the subject is "soil", the predicate is "has a type", the object is "chernozem". This approach allows you to organize queries in the language of descriptive logic.

In this paper, the Smart Grid ontology [3] is considered. Smart Grid is a new generation energy grid concept in which every consumer can act as a supplier. This aspect is achieved due to the introduction of alternative energy sources in the overall power supply scheme. The ontological model contains a description of the Smart Grid according to the IEC 61850 standard [4] and contains the main elements presented in the standard. This ontology was created on the basis of the top level CPS ontology [5]. The model contains both abstract concepts (Space, Rules, etc.) and concrete ones (SCL-description, IED, etc.).

Relational databases can be used to store the knowledge base. In [6], the ArchiGraph platform was developed, which allows accessing the knowledge base stored in relational databases using the SPARQL query interface and SHACL rules. One of its valuable features is the ability to change the set of physical data stores at runtime and redistribute data between them. But it is better to use Apache Jena FUSEKI [7], as this server is designed specifically for storing knowledge base. Article [8] highlights the benefits of the Apache Jena3 architecture and describes the Union, Intersection, and Difference operations.

In [9], two ontological models for a pharmacy and a clinic are created, which are combined into one model using Jena. The merged model is loaded into a Triple Store database created with the FUSEKI server. The database is queried using SPARQL to retrieve information about a doctor's prescription for a particular patient. In this work, unlike ours, it does not imply a change in the ontological model in the process of functioning.

In [10], two filters based on the SPARQL language are applied, which discard services that do not meet any of the functional requirements requested by the user. This improves the query speed. In our work, caching is used for such a task.

The article [11] developed an ontology for predicting diseases. The created ontology file is uploaded to the apache jena fuseki server. A SPARQL query with symptoms comes to the server, which is used to determine the disease. In this work, unlike ours, there is no mechanism for changing the ontology uploaded to the server.

For client-server interaction, the principle of the reader-writer task will be applied [12]. Writers priority, because any changes you make may change the results of the read requests that are executed.

Similar principles of work are shown in the article [13], the implementation of the reader-writer task is proposed, with the condition of priority of writers. Whenever a reader reads and when a writer enters the server to write, the existing reader process will pause execution and continue reading only when the writer process has completed. In our operation, write and read servers are separated, so the start of a write by a writer does not pause readers.

2 General Concept

Figure 1 shows the interaction diagram in the developed client-server architecture.

The client part is an application in which the user enters a request in the JSON language [14]. This language was chosen due to its vastness and unified data presentation. The entered request is sent to the server side, where it processes and returns a response to the client about the success or failure of the request.

The client consists of 3 main components:

1. Input module
    This module receives requests from users in the JSON language. Further, for this JSON request, the type of operation performed with the server is determined: reading (the request is sent to the "Reader") or writing (the request is sent to the "Writer").
2. Reading module
    This module generates a read request to the server based on a JSON request. SPARQL [15] or SQWRL [16] is chosen as the query language, depending on the dimension of the ontology or the type of query. A JSON query is converted to SPARQL or SQWRL using a translator. Next, read requests go to the cache server.
3. Recording module
    This module generates a write request to the server. OWL DL [17] or SWRL [18] is chosen as the query language, depending on the dimension of the ontology. A request from JSON is converted to OWL DL or SWRL using a translator. Next, write requests come to the recording server.

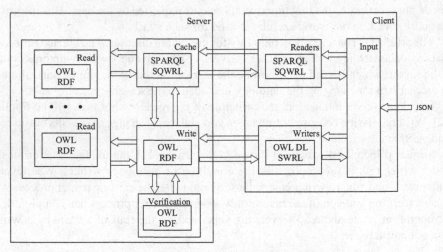

Fig. 1. General concept.

The server part is a set of several servers that process requests from many clients. A distributed knowledge base is also stored on the servers.

The server part consists of 4 main types of components:

1. CASH server
   This server stores the most frequent read requests and their responses. This allows you to reduce the number of calls directly to the knowledge base, which is located on the reading servers. The cache server is completely flushed when writing to the knowledge base for reading. If the current request is not in the list, then the CACHE server forwards the request further to the least loaded read server.
2. Reading module
   It can consist of any number of servers with the same information, which allows organizing data reading for several clients at once. The information on these servers is updated when an up-to-date knowledge base is received from the recording server. The response from the read server is fed back to the cache server. The knowledge bases on all servers are identical. Receiving requests may stop while the knowledge base is being updated from the recording server.
3. Recording server
   This server receives requests to modify the knowledge base. After modifying this server, the resulting model is verified. If the verification fails, then the correct database is read from one of the reading servers. After successful verification, the new state of the knowledge base is sent to all reading servers.
4. Verification module
   This module verifies the recording module after applying the changes received from the client. For example, a set of queries is checked, for which strictly defined answers must be obtained. The verification module can be either a separate server or a module as part of the recording server.

The algorithm of interaction between modules is as follows. The user writes a request in JSON in the client application. Depending on the type of request (read or write/modify), the Input application module sends a request to the writer or reader module. Let's start with a read request. In the reader of the client application, the query is converted using a translator into the SPARQL or SQWRL language. The converted request is sent to the cache server. If this request is in the list of cached requests, then the found response is sent to the user. If the request is not in the list of the CACHE server, then the request goes further to the least loaded reading server. On the read server, the request is processed and the found response is sent back to the cache server. On the cache server, the request is stored in the cache, and the response is sent to the user.

The write or change request will look like this. In the client application writer, the request is translated by a translator into OWL DL or SWRL. The transformed query (rule) is sent to the recording server. The knowledge base on the recording server is modified due to the received rule and a request for verification is received. The knowledge base on the recording server is verified based on the rules of the verification module. If the verification is not passed, then the knowledge base on the write server is restored from one of the read servers and a response is sent to the user about the failure of the write or modification. If the verification is successful, then all reading servers stop accepting requests while the knowledge base is being written from the writing server. After all read servers have been modified, a response about a successful write or modification is sent to the user.

3   Implementation Example

Consider the implementation of the interaction scheme for a limited system: only SPARQL will be used as a query language, and RDF will be used as an internal representation of the knowledge base. Apache Jena Fuseki was used as a tool.

As noted above, the Smart Grid ontology will be used as an example. The ontograph of this ontology is shown in Fig. 2.

This ontology presents a description of the Smart Grid in terms of not only physical properties, but also social engineering.

When a request is received from the user, the Input module analyzes it. If there is a DELETE or INSERT in the query, then the query is of type writers, if there is a SELECT statement, then it is of type readers. The incoming request interpreter is not universal and is created depending on the needs of the client, i.e. what operators, data, etc. can pass through it.

Let's consider examples of step-by-step execution of user scripts for two options: for reading and for modifying data.

1. Reading mode

The input is a JSON file with the following content:

```
{
"TypeObj": "subclass"
"TypeMain": "human"
"Type": "SELECT"
}
```

This query can be interpreted as follows: find all "human" that will be subclasses of the "human" class.

After receiving the submitted JSON file as input, the type of its content is analyzed. In the example, the type is SELECT, so the query will be directed to the readers module.

On the reader module, the dimension of the ontological model is checked on the server side. This value is obtained from the cache. This is necessary due to the fact that different types of queries have different performance dependencies when accessing ontologies of different dimensions. In this implementation, we will consider the use of a query in the SPARQL language. Thus, the source file in JSON format will be converted on the client into a request to the ontological model of the following form:

PREFIX rdf: <http://www.w3.org/1999/02/22-rdf-syntax-ns#>
PREFIX owl: <http://www.w3.org/2002/07/owl#>
PREFIX rdfs: <http://www.w3.org/2000/01/rdf-schema#>
PREFIX xsd: <http://www.w3.org/2001/XMLSchema#>
PREFIX ow: <http://www.semanticweb.org/untitled-ontology-74#>
SELECT ?subject
    WHERE { ?subject rdfs:subClassOf ow:Human}

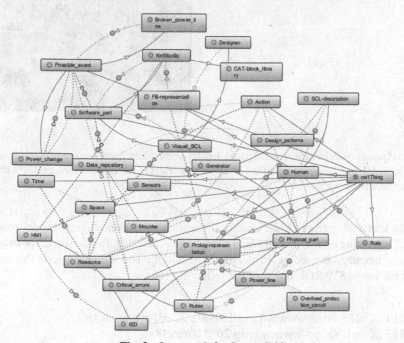

Fig. 2. Ontograph for Smart Grid.

At the next stage, this request goes to the caching module on the client. If this request was found in the cache, then the answer will also be taken from the cache. If this request is not found in the cache, then a group of reading servers is accessed, and the request will be executed on the least loaded reading server.

Figure 3 shows the response from the read server.

2. Write request.

The input of the Input module receives a JSON file with the following content.

```
{
    "TypeObj": "subclass"
    "TypeMain": "human"
    "Type": "INSERT"
    "New": "testProperty"
}
```

This file is a request like: add a testProperty object as a subclass of the human class. The INPUT module analyzes this file and determines that the type of operation is the introduction of new data into the ontological model. So it redirects the file to the writer.

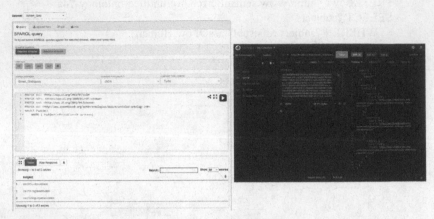

Fig. 3. Request and response from Apache Fuseki server. The figure on the left is represented through the UI directly by Apache Fuseki, and on the right is through the Rest protocol through the Insomnia client application.

The writer also requests the current dimension of the ontological model from the client. Depending on the size, the query language is selected. In this work, for example, the same language is used as for reading – SPARQL. The writer converts the original JSON file into a SPARQL query of the following form:

PREFIX rdf: <http://www.w3.org/1999/02/22-rdf-syntax-ns#>
PREFIX owl: <http://www.w3.org/2002/07/owl#>
PREFIX rdfs: <http://www.w3.org/2000/01/rdf-schema#>
PREFIX xsd: <http://www.w3.org/2001/XMLSchema#>
PREFIX ow: <http://www.semanticweb.org/артём/ontologies/2022/4/untitled-ontology-74#>
INSERT {
  ow:testProperty rdfs:subClassOf ow:Human
} where {}

The recording server, upon receiving a request from a client, applies it to a copy of the ontological model stored inside this module. Then the resulting ontology is passed to the validation module.

The validation module checks the ontology for logical errors (for example, adding an object that is already in the ontology as a subclass) as well as restrictions introduced by the user (for example, prohibiting the creation of subclasses or limiting their number). If the validation process ended with an error, then a 422 code is sent to the client, and the ontology itself on the module is rolled back to the changes (for this, the ontology is read from the reader server. If the validation is successful, the ontology from the writer module is broadcast to all readers, and the read cache is reset.

Figure 4 shows the result of the query execution. When requesting to read all subclasses of the Human class, the added entry is at the end of the list.

As an example of a write request, a new subclass was added to the Human class.

Also, using a write request, you can remove any triplet from the knowledge base. To do this, you need to specify the DELETE operator instead of the INSERT operator.

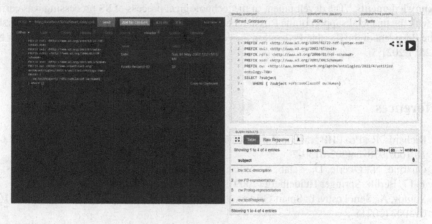

Fig. 4. Adding an entry and checking that the entry has been added. The figure on the left shows a request to add an entry – via the Rest protocol through the Insomnia client application, and on the right, a request to read the added entry through the UI directly from Apache Fuseki.

4 Conclusion

This paper presents the concept of a client-server architecture of the knowledge base, which has the following advantages:

- Parallel execution – the number of clients, theoretically, can be as many as you like for read operations, for a write operation there can be only one client at a time.
- Distribution – at a minimum, separate servers for reading, writing and verification, between which synchronization occurs periodically.
- Verification (to protect against failures) – after updating the recording server, the verification server will receive a request to check the correct operation after the changes. If the check is passed, then the data from the write server will be rewritten to the read server, if not, then the previous version is considered from the read server to the write server.
- Polymorphism (support for different types of received data) – translation of queries into a modified language (SPARQL or SQWRL) depending on the dimension of the ontology.

– Scalability – the number of reading servers can be increased or decreased depending on the load.
– Caching – saving the result of a frequently used query. Upon successful write, the cache is reset.

In further studies, it is planned to implement the general concept based on data on the speed of execution of individual types of queries for different languages.

Acknowledgments. The development of the technological process of SS processing was carried out with the financial support of the Russian Federation President Council on Grants (scholarship of the President of the Russian Federation for young scientists and graduate students) (project No. SP-2511.2021.5).

References

1. Richards, R.: Pro PHP XML and web services. Apress, Berkeley, CA (2006). https://doi.org/10.1007/978-1-4302-0139-7
2. Guarino, N., Oberle, D., Staab, S.: What is an ontology? In: Handbook on ontologies, pp 1–17. Berlin: Springer Heidelberg (2009)
3. Voinov, A., Senokosov, I.: Smart Grid model verification method. J. Phys: Conf. Ser. **2001**(1), 012003 (2021)
4. IEC 61850 - Communication networks and systems for power utility automation, IEC Standard, Part 6: Configuration language for communication in electrical substations related to IEDs, Ed 2 (2009)
5. Voinov, A., Senokosov, I.: Ontological models of cyber physical systems. J. Phys: Conf. Ser. **1889**(2), 022064 (2021)
6. Gorshkov S., Grebeshkov A., Shebalov, R.: Ontology-based industrial data management platform arXiv:2103.05538 (2021)
7. Apache jena fuseki: The apache software foundation, 18 (2014)
8. Mutawalli, L., Suhriani, I., Supardianto, S.: Implementasi SPARQL dengan framework Jena Fuseki untuk melakukan pencarian pengetahuan pada model ontologi jalur klinis tata laksana perawatan penyakit katarak. Jurnal Informatika dan Rekayasa Elektronik **1**(2), 68–75 (2018)
9. Sigwele, T., et al.: Building a Semantic RESTFul API for Achieving Interoperability between a Pharmacist and a Doctor using Jena and Fuseki. J. Phys: Conf. Ser. **1376**(1), 012015 (2019)
10. Thapar, P., Sharma, L.S.: Implementing SPARQL-based Prefiltering on Jena Fuseki TDB store to reduce the semantic web services search space. In: Suma, V., Fernando, X., Du, K.-L., Wang, H. (eds.) Evolutionary Computing and Mobile Sustainable Networks. LNDECT, vol. 116, pp. 319–333. Springer, Singapore (2022). https://doi.org/10.1007/978-981-16-9605-3_22
11. Raju, S., Snehaja, K., Srinivas, B.: Ontology based disease prediction system. In: 2021 6th International Conference on Communication and Electronics Systems (ICCES), pp. 1–6, IEEE (2021)
12. Greif, I.: Formal problem specifications for readers and writers scheduling. Proc. MRI Symp. Comptr. Software Eng. (1976)
13. Sreejith, S., et al.: Distributed readers writer problem: extending to pause, resume, and stop functionality. In: 2020 4th International Conference on Trends in Electronics and Informatics (ICOEI), pp. 635–638. IEEE (2020)

14. Sporny, M., et al.: JSON-LD 1.0, W3C recommendation **16**, 41 (2014)
15. Pérez, J., Arenas, M., Gutierrez, C.: Semantics and complexity of SPARQL. ACM Trans. Database Syst. (TODS) **34**(3), 1–45 (2009)
16. O'Connor, M., Das, A.: SQWRL: a query language for OWL, pp. 1–8. OWLED529 (2009)
17. Motik, B., Sattler, U., Studer, R.: Query answering for OWL-DL with rules. In: McIlraith, S.A., Plexousakis, D., van Harmelen, F. (eds.) ISWC 2004. LNCS, vol. 3298, pp. 549–563. Springer, Heidelberg (2004). https://doi.org/10.1007/978-3-540-30475-3_38
18. Horrocks, I., Patel-Schneider, P., Boley, H., Tabet, S., Grosof, B., Dean, M.: SWRL: a semantic web rule language combining OWL and RuleML. W3C Member Submission **21**(79), 1–31 (2004)

Experimental Study of Russian-Language News Text Categorization Performance Using Machine Learning Algorithms

Eduard Chelyshev[1]([✉]) [iD], Shamil Otsokov[1] [iD], Marina Raskatova[1] [iD],
Pavel Shchegolev[1] [iD], and Lyudmila Sharapova[2] [iD]

[1] National Research University "Moscow Power Engineering Institute", 14,
Krasnokazarmennaya Street, Moscow 111250, Russian Federation
chel.ed@yandex.ru
[2] Russian New University, 22, Radio Street, Moscow 105005, Russian Federation

Abstract. Text categorization is one of the fields of natural language processing. The relevance of the research is due to the really large demand for automatic text categorization means for real-time processing of the content in news resources and social networks. It is necessary to note that the volume of such content grows at a high rate. The article considers the problem of Russian-language news text categorization. An algorithm of text preprocessing is proposed. The feature generation was performed using vector space model FastText. The following machine learning methods were used: Naive Bayes, Random Forest, Logistic Regression and Artificial Neural Network. The research was carried out on the Russian-language corpus of documents related to the nine following topics: Home, Internet and Media, Culture, Science and Technology, Politics, Journeys, Military Structures, Sport, Economics and Business. The classification quality of the trained classification models has been evaluated using a number of performance measures: precision, recall and F1-score.

Keywords: Text categorization · Classification · Text preprocessing · Feature generation · Classification performance measure

1 Introduction

There is a large amount of text data contained in the Internet: news articles, publications in social networks, scientific papers, etc. The permanently growing volume of text data prompts to search different ways for text systematization. For this reason the investigation of text document categorization methods is an important domain of natural language processing. The text categorization is a form of the multiclass classification task. This paper contains a possible algorithm of text data preprocessing and comparative analysis of some classification methods in reference to the solution of Russian-language news text categorization task.

A. Gibadullin (Ed.): ITIDMS 2021, CCIS 1703, pp. 138–147, 2022.
https://doi.org/10.1007/978-3-031-21340-3_13

2 Related Work

There are a lot of works dedicated to solving the problem of news text categorization in various languages using different machine learning methods. For example, the paper [1] evaluates the performance of five classification models on the English-language news BBC corpus. The Naive Bayes, Support Vector Machine, Multilayer Perceptron Neural Network, Random Forest and Decision Tree are considered in the article in question. TF-IDF method is used for feature selection. The best classification quality in this article was shown by Naive Bayes. The value of accuracy in the work under consideration is equal to 96.8%.

The cross-validation procedure based approach to text feature selection is investigated in the research [2]. The following classification models were applied for news text classification: Support Vector Machine, Naive Bayes and Logistic Regression. The models were tested on three text corpora: 1) Data1 that contains text documents related to four topics: "Women", "Sports", "Literature", "Campus"; 2) Data2 that includes topics: "Sports", "Constellation", "Game", "Entertainment"; 3) Data3 that is categorized into topics: "Science and Technology", "Fashion", "Current Event". The best classification quality for the Data1 and Data2 corpora was obtained using Support Vector Machine. The values of F1-score for the Data1 and Data2 corpora are equal to 0.86 and 0.71, respectively. The best classification quality for the Data3 corpus was reached using Logistic Regression. In this case the value of F1-score is equal to 0.63.

The article [3] also evaluates the performance of the classification models on the BBC corpus containing news text documents related to five topics: "Business", "Entertainment", "Politics", "Sports" and "Tech". In the paper in question the following classifiers were utilized: Naive Bayes, Support Vector Machine, Logistic Regression, Decision Tree and Random Forest. The TF-IDF method is used for the feature selection. The highest classification quality was obtained using Logistic Regression. The value of the accuracy is equal to 95.5%.

There are a number of researches dedicated to the application of neural networks for solving the news text classification problem. For example, Deep Learning Convolutional Neural Network is used to solve the problem under consideration in [4]. The author performed text feature selection using the TF-IDF method. Four corpora are used: DBMC-1, DBMC-2, DBMC-3 and DBMC-4, every of them are categorized into three topics. The obtained value of the accuracy for developed Convolutional Neural Network is more than 90% and appears better than the same value for some other methods considered in the paper.

The paper [5] studies the question of the text feature selection. The author proposes an original method for the text feature selection and compares its information expression ability with some other methods: the vector space model, the chi-square test and the TF-IDF method. It is shown that the proposed method demonstrates the best result. The following classification models are utilized in the work: Multilayer Perceptron, Convolutional Neural Network, Long Short-Term Memory and others. The value of the accuracy reaches 94.82%.

There are a number of researches on the news text classification problem for other languages different from English. For example, the problem in question is solved for the Arabic language. The paper [6] considers C4.5, Naive Bayes and Discriminative parameter learning for Bayesian network for text (DMNBtext) as classifiers. The paper also contains an investigation of the influence of text preprocessing on the classification quality: three stemming approaches and twelve methods of term weighting are studied in the article under consideration. The authors use two Arabic-language corpora: the corpus from the BBC website, containing the news texts related to seven topics, and the corpus collected from the CNN website, containing the news texts from six topics. The result demonstrates that the highest performance comparatively with other considered methods was achieved for the DMNBtext classification method.

The paper [7] is dedicated to solving the problem of the Russian-language news text categorization. Preprocessing of text documents includes removal of html tags and stop words. The feature selection is performed using the TF-IDF method. Some different numbers of features taken into account were tried: 0.01 N, 0.05 N, 0.1 N, 0.25 N, 0.5 N and N, where N is a total number of features in the training corpus. For every number of features the following methods were trained and tested: Logistic Regression, Light Gradient Boosted Machine, k-Nearest Neighbors, Random Forest, Naive Bayes, Support Vector Machine and Bidirectional Encoder Representations from Transformers, pretrained on Russian Wikipedia and news articles (RuBERT). The text corpus was formed from news articles, every one of them belongs to one of six topics: "Culture", "Economics", "Sports", "Society", "Accidents" and "Politics". Two classification models showed the highest quality: RuBERT with N features and Support Vector Machine with 0.1 N features. Average values of F1-score for every model were equal to 0.882 and 0.877, respectively.

This article has the following differences from the works mentioned above: 1) an algorithm of text preprocessing and its implementation are described; 2) the feature generation was performed using the vector space model FastText.

3 Materials and Methods

3.1 Method for Solving the Problem of News Text Categorization

The given solution of the problem of the Russian-language news text categorization consists of the following stages:

1. Text preprocessing.
2. Feature generation.
3. Training the classification models.
4. Evaluation the classification quality.

3.2   A Subsection Sample

The text corpus used was taken from the Internet news portal "Lenta.ru" for the period from 1999 to 2019. It contains news articles belonging to the nine topics: "Home", "Internet and Media", "Culture", "Science and Technology", "Politics", "Journeys", "Military Structures", "Sports", "Economics and Business". The distribution of the news articles by the topics is presented in Table 1.

Table 1. Distribution of news articles by topics

Topic	Number of documents
Home	21,734
Internet and media	44,663
Culture	53,796
Science and technology	53,136
Politics	40,716
Journeys	6,408
Military structures	19,596
Sport	64,413
Economics and business	86,926

The text corpus under consideration is imbalanced. The largest topic "Economics and Business" contains 86,926 documents. The smallest topic "Journeys" contains 6,408 documents which is more than 13 times less than the number of the documents in the previous topic.

3.3   Text Preprocessing and Feature Generation

Text preprocessing includes the following steps: the removal of irrelevant characters and casting to a common register, the tokenization, the removal of stop words and the normalization Ошибка! Источник ссылки не найден.. The program unit in the Python programming language for the preprocessing implementation has been developed.

All the non-alphabetical characters excluding spaces are considered as irrelevant. The removal of irrelevant characters and casting to a common register were implemented using the regular expressions. The URL links presented in the text were also removed. Tokenization is the process of splitting text into terms that is words. Text of each document in the corpus was split into separate terms.

Normalization is the process of transforming a word into its canonical form. It can be very important in languages that have a rich morphological structure like Russian. Normalization reduces the noise induced by the words with multiple grammatical forms. There are two approaches to the text normalization: stemming and lemmatization. Stemming is the process of reducing a word to its stem or root format. Lemmatization is the process of transformation of a term that uses a dictionary to map a grammatical form to the normal form of the word, or lemma. The lemmatization approach chosen for the text normalization in the current work was performed using the Russian-language morphological analyzer implemented in the pymorphy2 library Ошибка! Источник ссылки не найден..

Stop words are the words that are often found in text like particles, prepositions, conjunctions, pronouns, etc. They play a significant role in providing sentence coherence, but they are considered as a noise in natural language processing. The problem of the stop words removal was solved using the NLTK library of the Python programming language.

The feature generation problem was solved using the FastText vector space model Ошибка! Источник ссылки не найден.. The realization of the FastText vector space model used in the work was pretrained on the Russian-language GeoWAC corpus. The generated vector representations of terms have the dimension equal to 300. The vector representation of a document was calculated as the average vector representation for every term in the document.

3.4   A Subsection Sample

The experiments were conducted using the Python programming language. The following machine learning classification methods were used for text categorization: Naive Bayes (NB), Random Forest (RF), Logistic Regression (LR) and Artificial Neural Network (ANN). The software implementation of NB, RF and LR were taken from the scikit-learn library Ошибка! Источник ссылки не найден.. The ANN was implemented using the Keras library Ошибка! Источник ссылки не найден..

The structure of the developed ANN is depicted in Fig. 1. The input dense layer contains 300 neurons each for a corresponding coordinate of a 300-dimensional vector representation of a considered document. The first hidden layer is a Dropout layer which disables some of its neurons while training in order to prevent overfitting. The second hidden layer is a BatchNormalization layer that provides statistical normalization of the values obtained from the outputs of the previous layers. The output layer has 9 neurons one for every topic. The ReLU function was used as an activation function for the hidden layers. The activation function of the output layer is Softmax, which is a multidimensional generalization of the logistic function.

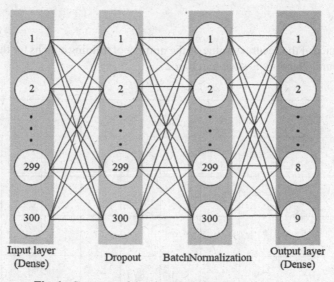

Fig. 1. Structure of developed artificial neural network

For the evaluation of the classification quality, the following performance measures were used: precision, recall and F1-score. Precision and recall are calculated using formulae (1) and (2), respectively.

$$P = \frac{TP}{TP + FP} \tag{1}$$

$$R = \frac{TP}{TP + FN} \tag{2}$$

where TP is the number of objects that were correctly classified as the ones that belong to this class; FP is the number of objects that were mistakenly classified as the ones that belong to this class; FN is the number of objects that were mistakenly classified as the ones that don't belong to this class.

The F-score can be used as a combined classification performance measure. It is determined in accordance with the formula (3), where the parameter β has the meaning of the precision weight.

$$F_\beta = (1 + \beta^2) \frac{P \cdot R}{\beta^2 \cdot P + R} \tag{3}$$

A special case of the F-score is the one when β = 1. F1-score was used for evaluating the classification performance.

4 Results

The dependence of the accuracy value on the number of training epochs for the developed Artificial Neural Network is shown in Fig. 2.

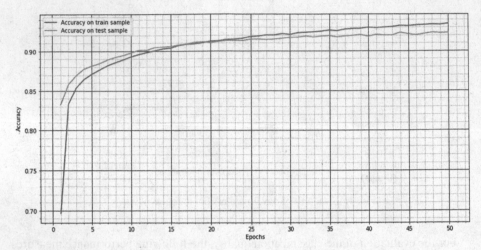

Fig. 2. Dependence of the accuracy value on the number of training epochs

Average values of precision, recall and F1-score, obtained for every classification model while testing, are presented in Table 2 and Fig. 3.

Table 2. Classification performance

Classification method	Average value of precision	Average value of recall	Average value of F1-score
Naive Bayes	0.8146	0.7978	0.7537
Logistic regression	0.9022	0.9024	0.9022
Random forest	0.8832	0.8831	0.8822
Neural network	0.9253	0.9250	0.9251

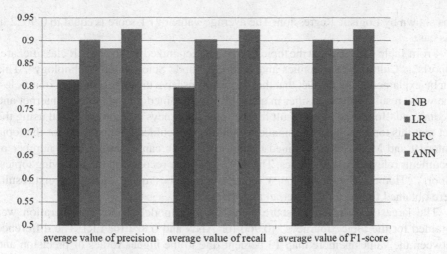

Fig. 3. Average values of performance measures for every classification model

The values of the performance measures for two leading classification models calculated for every topic are presented in Table 3.

Table 3. Performance measures of LR and ANN calculated for every topic

Topic	Logistic regression			Artificial neural network		
	Precision	Recall	F1-score	Precision	Recall	F1-score
Home	0.874	0.849	0.862	0.959	0.9241	0.941
Internet and media	0.829	0.812	0.820	0.868	0.883	0.876
Culture	0.929	0.936	0.932	0.943	0.931	0.937
Science and technology	0.909	0.905	0.907	0.918	0.901	0.909
Politics	0.858	0.873	0.866	0.883	0.912	0.897
Journeys	0.834	0.823	0.829	0.955	0.965	0.960
Military structures	0.851	0.837	0.844	0.919	0.934	0.927
Sport	0.979	0.977	0.978	0.977	0.986	0.982
Economics and business	0.907	0.918	0.913	0.903	0.891	0.897

5   Discussion

Analysis of Table 2 shows that the ANN classification model demonstrates the best result among all four classifiers considered. The average values of precision, recall and F1-score for ANN are equal to 0.9253, 0.9250 and 0.9251, respectively. The second result was shown by Logistic Regression. The average value of F1-score is equal to 0.9022 in this case.

From Table 3 follows that the topics that were recognized best by the LR classifier are: "Sports", "Culture", "Economics and Business" and "Science and Technology". This can be explained using the fact that these four topics have the largest number of articles. The worst result for the classifier in question was obtained for the topics: "Internet and Media" and "Journeys". This result for the topic "Journeys" can be explained using the fact that this topic includes the smallest number of documents. This result for the topic "Internet and Media" was obtained because this topic can contain a large number of documents relevant to other topics. The ANN classifier recognized the following topics: "Sport", "Home", "Journeys" and "Culture" with the best quality, and the worst results were obtained for the topic "Internet and Media".

The largest gap in the F1-score value for two models under consideration was obtained for the topic "Journeys" (0.960 for ANN and 0.829 for LR). The difference between the values is more than 13 percent due to the higher values of precision and recall. It is important to note that LR showed the higher classification quality for the topic "Economics and Business". The values of all performance measures for LR are more than the same values for ANN in the current topic (for example, the difference between the values of F1-score for LR and ANN is more than 1 percent). The higher values for precision were demonstrated by the LR classifier for topics: "Sport" and "Economics and Business". The LR classifier gives the highest values of recall for the topics: "Culture", "Science and Technology" and "Economics and Business". The ANN classifier demonstrates higher results in all other cases.

6 Conclusion

Text categorization is an important task of natural language processing and has a significant practical value. The problem under consideration can be solved using machine learning methods. This work experimentally investigates the Russian-language news text categorization performance. The following classification algorithms were used: Naive Bayes, Logistic Regression, Random Forest and Artificial Neural Network.

The highest classification quality was demonstrated by the Artificial Neural Network. The value of F1-score for it is equal to 0.9251. The second result was obtained using Logistic Regression (F1-score is equal to 0.9022). The topics "Sports" and "Culture" were recognized using both leading classification models with the highest quality, the topic "Internet and Media" is the most difficult for recognition by models under consideration.

It is planned to investigate other classification models for the task of Russian-language news text categorization in future works. It is also planned to study the training time consumed by those models and the amount of memory required for the trained classification models.

References

1. Deb, N., Jha, V., Panjiyar, A., Gupta, R.: A comparative analysis of news categorization using machine learning approaches. Int. J. Sci. Technol. Res. **9**(1), 2469–2472 (2020)
2. Luo, X.: Efficient English text classification using selected machine learning techniques. Alex. Eng. J. **60**(3), 3401–3409 (2021)
3. Patro, A., Patel, M., Shukla, R., Save, J.: Real time news classification using machine learning. Int. J. Adv. Sci. Technol. **29**(9), 620–630 (2020)
4. Zhu, Y.: Research on news text classification based on deep learning convolutional neural network. Wirel. Commun. Mob. Comput. (2021). https://doi.org/10.1155/2021/1508150
5. Zhang, M.: Applications of deep learning in news text classification. Sci. Program. (2021). https://doi.org/10.1155/2021/6095354
6. Alshammari, R.: Arabic text categorization using machine learning approaches. Int. J. Adv. Comput. Sci. Appl. **9**(3), 226–230 (2018)
7. Vychegzhanin, S., Kotelnikov, E., Milov, V.: Comparative analysis of machine learning methods for news categorization in Russian. In: Proceedings of the II International Scientific and Practical Conference "Information Technologies and Intelligent Decision Making Systems" (ITIDMS-II-2021), Moscow, Russian Federation, pp. 100–108. CEUR Workshop Proceedings, Aachen, Germany (2021)
8. Hartmann, J., Huppertz, J., Schamp, C., Heitmann, M.: Comparing automated text classification methods. Int. J. Res. Mark. **36**, 20–38 (2019)
9. Korobov, M.: Morphological analyzer and generator for Russian and Ukrainian languages. In: Analysis of Images, Social Networks and Texts, pp. 320–332 (2015)
10. Korogodina, O., Karpik, O., Klyshinsky, E.S.: Evaluation of vector transformations for Russian Word2Vec and FastText Embeddings. In: Proceedings of the 30th International Conference on Computer Graphics and Machine Vision (GraphiCon 2020), Saint Petersburg, Russian Federation. CEUR Workshop Proceedings, Aachen, Germany (2020)
11. Pedregosa, F., et al.: Scikit-learn: machine learning in python. J. Mach. Learn. Res. **12**, 2825–2830 (2011)
12. Chollet, F.: Keras: the python deep learning library. Astrophysics Source Code Library (2018)

Author Index

Printed in the United States
by Baker & Taylor Publisher Services

Printed in the United States
by Baker & Taylor Publisher Services